JOURNALISTS AS PUBLIC INTELLECTUAL

A STUDY OF PUBLIC INTELLECTUALISM OF GOPABANDHU DAS AND SURENDRA MOHANTY AS PART OF PRE-INDEPENDENCE AND POST-INDEPENDENCE ODISHA

PADMALOCHAN SAHU

Dedicated...

Dedicated to the creator of great heart of mine, my honest father and
my dear love, my innocent mother.

"Some histories and some great personalities are visible

And some are invisible

And some are ignored

But you are unknown

To the world of documentation and evidence...

Here I am your production of great heart

And rare innocence

And the world can see you my both love

Through the quality you transferred and

I received heartly as a big drop from the hidden sea...

And I am waiting to meet you again and

Hug you forever eternally..."

My Mother and Father

Contents

Preface

There are many books available on Journalists, on public intellectuals but a good book on journalists who are public intellectuals especially in Odisha is still hard to find. I have taken two public intellectuals; **Gopabandhu Das** from Pre-Independent India/Odisha and **Surendra Mohanty** from Post-Independent India/Odisha to study them with two different societies of India; Pre-Independent Society of Odisha and Post-Independent Society of Odisha. My study is centered and narrowed to **Gopabandhu Das** and **Surendra Mohanty** with their societies and times. Covering Pre-Independent Odisha and Post-Independent Odisha is a matter of huge research and observation which is not covered by this book. It just focusses on two journalists and their public activities as they are public intellectuals and their connections with their time. This book was primarily a research paper by me during my **M.Phil.** Degree. I got to realise that my valuable research paper became valueless after completion of my degree. I with some extra-effort developed it into a book.

I finally got a valuable and interesting topic after rejection of two research ideas and after a long discussion with my peers and supervisor. My interest in journalism led to my current topic. I would like to thank my supervisor **Shaswat Panda** for going through my drafts and offering valuable suggestions. My heartfelt thanks to **Animesh Mohapatra** who is also a professor of English literature at **Delhi College of Arts and Commerce, University of Delhi,** with whom I had important discussions on public sphere in Odisha. I also got the valuable advice from Professor **Pritish Acharya** (a renowned historian and writer from Odisha) and from **Mrinal Chatterjee** (journalist and chairman of IIMC, Dhenkanal). I am deeply indebted to these two academicians who despite their profound insights, wear their scholarship lightly. I am also grateful to **Sisir Behera** (prof. of Odia literature, North Orissa University and **Sahitya Academy** Awardee) who gave me easy access to archival resources, and arranged meetings with scholars and journalists. I also got the opportunity to meet **Gourahari Das** (a renowned litterateur and journalist from Odisha). Gourahari sir gave me valuable advice and helped me to access and collect my material from the library of *The Sambad* newspaper (a popular and successful newspaper of Odisha). I cannot thank him enough. I thank them from the bottom of my heart.

With the moral inspiration of **Bikash Chandra Behera**, (Assistant Professor, Department of English, **D.D. Autonomous College, Keonjhar**) on book writing, I decided to work on this book more seriously. I could not proceed and finish my writing but for the valuable help of the above-mentioned individuals. Thank you so much to all.

A meeting with Gourahari Sir (A renowned author of Odisha, India) at Sambad office, Bhubaneswar

Enter Caption Collected old writings of Surendra Mohanty from Sambad News Paper library.

Enter Caption

Prologue

Introduction

In this book, it is asserted that the notion or idea of public intellectual changes time to time. Society structure changes according to the change of time. Society structures and various factors work as the force for the various works and actions of a public intellectual. According to the advancement of time various things such as rise of bourgeois or middle class, invention of printing machine, running of newspapers, increase of public discussion and public sphere etc., change the notion and style of public intellectual. The notion 'time' is not confined with time only. It is more connected with different situations, conditions and society structure of the contemporary society or the society under study. It takes two public intellectuals of two different time such as Gopabandhu Das from Pre-Independent time and Surendra Mohanty from Post-Independent time. I discuss both public intellectuals with their time structures. The field of knowledge or profession has a major role in the works of a public intellectual to which we can find in the case of Das and Mohanty. Above all, works and actions of a public intellectual largely get the shape by the society structure of him/her and he/she never help himself/herself to stay away from the social structures and factors of his/her time and can never be total autonomous.

The term 'public intellectual' is a modern term which first gained currency in **America**. The tradition of public intellectual is not new and we cannot be certain about the particular time of its origin. **Hellen Small** in her book ***The Public Intellectual***says , "The term 'public intellectual' is a fairly recent addition to the vocabulary of cultural debate."(Small 1) And at the same page she mentions that, "Having first gained currency in the United States a little over a decade ago, the phrase caught on in **Britain** comparatively slowly and has only entered common usage within the last two or three years."(1) One might say that it was particularly during these years that the term resurfaced in public discourse but to argue altogether that it originated during those years would be unfair to the long tradition of public intellectuals and also historically inaccurate.

The term might have originated in America but the tradition has no accurate claim of origin. The concept 'public intellectual' consist of two words: public and intellectual. Public means a group of people who are counted for some common points or issues. Intellectual means a man who is endowed with intellect and is a concerned thinker. **Collins Dictionary** defines the meaning of 'public intellectual' as, "**an intellectual often a noted specialist in particular field, who has become well known to the general public for a willingness to comment on current affairs.**" Oxford Dictionary describes this as, "**An intellectual who express views (especially on popular topics) intended to be accessible to a general audience.**" From above definition we can understand that public intellectuals are intellect persons who communicate their thought with people or public. Public intellectual is not a profession. A public intellectual may belong to any kind of field. Most of the public intellectuals deal the issues related with their profession. A professor of English literature can deal with issues of English literature more comfortably because he/she has better knowledge on that field than other profession people. We also can say that public intellectual concerns herself/himself with issues that are of interest to the public. Sometimes public find the opinion of public intellectuals unacceptable. Public intellectuals always target a public and try to communicate their thoughts with that public. Many directly reveal the truth and share those to clear the confusion of people. Public intellectuals are known to follow logical and critical process of thought and are rarely irrational. The reason behind this might be the evolution of the tradition of public intellectuals during Enlightenment which marshalled reason and critical thinking as its greatest virtues. Many intellectuals think and discuss social and political issues but a public intellectual not only thinks but also communicates his/her thought with people.

An academician who communicates his thought through his speech, TV channels and newspapers, can be called a public intellectual. A journalist or columnist who shares his thoughts with people through journalistic writings, we can call him a public intellectual. But every journalist need not necessarily be a public intellectual. A journalist can deal with every type of issues and matters in the world. But a journalist would qualify as an intellectual who deals with issues related with a public and writes journalistic writings for that public. The emergence of the public intellectual (as we understand it today) is a modern phenomenon for many reasons. A typically modern phenomenon which accounts for the rise of the public intellectual was the invention of the printing press which brought about a revolution in the world. Because of this innovation, making of newspaper and book in a rapid speed became possible and a revolution came in the field of information and knowledge. Printing press was invented in 1439 in Europe. Then this machine was advanced technologically. It came to India during 16th century. In India newspaper printing began in 18th century. The first newspaper of India was the English newspaper titled *Bengal Gazette* published by the British man **James Augustus Hicky** in March 23, 1782 from Calcutta (which was the capital of India during British rule). In Odisha, British missionaries established a printing press in **1837** in Cuttack which was known as *Cuttack Missionaries Press*. They started by printing pamphlets on **Rathayatra** of Odisha to garner the attention of the Hindus of Odisha but the document was printed in English. In 1866, *Budha Dayini* started from Balasore as the first magazine of Odisha. In the same year **Gouri Shankar Ray** started the *Utkal Dipika* newspaper which was the first newspaper of Odisha which was in Odia language. From that time, journey of newspaper establishment started. The weekly newspaper *Sambad Vahika*started in 1868, the *Utkal Hiteisini*in 1869 etc., many newspapers and journals came out continually.

The nature and tradition of public intellectual has been changing time to time. The structure of society changes and differs in different time. We also cannot deny the role of society and time to produce a public intellectual. The historian **Pritish Acharya** in his introduction to *Gopabandhu Chayanika* says that **Gopabandhu** and **Gandhi** can be seen as products of their time and society. It means if Gandhi would not have been born in that time, he might not have able to do the kind of work which made him famous; similarly, Gopabandhu also might not have done the same job if he came out in later world. It is also true that society and time would have given the name of 'Mahatma' to another person in the absence of Gandhi and would have constructed another **'Utkalamani'** (Jewel of Odisha) in the absence of Gopabandhu. Changing system of society would not have stopped by the lack of their present. **Hellen Small** describes this in her book *The Public Intellectual*that

The level of alarm differs, of course, as does the sense of what, if anything, needs to be done, but there is some agreement that an explanation is to be found in a series of structural changes across the course of the twentieth century which have fundamentally affected the ways in which we conceive of the public domain and the kinds of influence that the public intellectual can therefore wield. (Small Hellen 2)

As I have discussed before, public intellectuals are intellectuals who raise the issues related to contemporary public. But they raise the issues in a manner which are beneficial for people not harmful. But in present day, it is so much hard to differentiate between 'intellectual' in general and 'public intellectual' because of modernization of social institutions and because of the presence of innumerable newspapers, T.V channels, web news, mass media, internet system etc. Many people are gaining popularity and public recognition through these platforms. Many people speak on public issues through these media and it creates confusion. But we also cannot ignore the change of the social structure and notion of public intellectual due to change of time. To know a public intellectual, we must study his/her social structure and the connection of the issues and opinions discussed by him/her by his writing or speech with the contemporary society.

Newspapers and journals are the most used medium by public intellectuals. After the circulation of newspapers and journals in Odisha, many intellectuals communicated their thought with people through these mediums. Newspapers were the successful medium during the freedom struggle in India and in Odisha. Many social workers and leaders of freedom struggle used this medium to succeed in their motive, and one of them was **Gopabandhu Das**. He used the medium of newspaper to achieve his success in social works and freedom movements. He was an important intellectual of Odisha and we can call him as a journalist public intellectual because he communicated with people by using the medium of journalism.

In this research paper in first chapter, it started the discussion from understanding the notion 'public' then 'public sphere' and then 'public intellectual'. These discussions are important to understand the notion of public intellectual. The term 'public' is common in both public sphere and public intellectual. These three notions are related with each other. Public means a group of people who are counted for some similar things. There is a little difference between public discussions and public sphere. People can discuss any important or unimportant topic which form parts of public discussion. Public sphere is a term coined by Jurgen Habermas; it is also a public discussion but this discussion is a critical public discussion on social issues which often affect system and government to change policy. Public discussion, public sphere and public intellectual are related with each other. In a society sometimes, some people lead a public for discussion and for social change to whom we call public intellectual and sometimes some public leaders or public intellectuals come out by getting inspiration from public discussions or public spheres. In this way, these notions are related with each other. There is no strong proof using which we can attribute the root cause to any one of these notions. After the invention of printing press and after the beginning and circulation of newspapers the system of public sphere and quantity of public intellectual rapidly increased. Because of newspapers, many people gained good knowledge on practical matters and other issues by which the number of intellectual grew and because intellectuals shared their logical and critical views to society through newspapers, people gained a logical and critical view point by which public sphere grew in different societies among people. We cannot give total credit to public intellectuals for the creation of public sphere or we also cannot give total credit to newspapers for public sphere and public intellectual creation. Both newspapers and public intellectuals help to create and sustain public sphere and public intellectuals in society.

To study Gopabandhu Das and Surendra Mohanty as journalists and public intellectuals, we must know the social structure and social issues of their times and the connection of these with their journal writings. The life period of Gopabandhu Das was from 1877 to 1928 and of Surendra Mohanty was from 1922 to 1990.They both were from Odisha but they both lived in different society and different time and both are different from profession. Because Gopabandhu Das lived earlier than Surendra Mohanty, it will start the exploration from Gopabandhu Das. The contemporary situation of Gopabandhu Das, especially the time of his journalistic writings is essential to understand him as public intellectual. It is essential in the sense that a public intellectual deal with the issues and other social structures related to public of his time and his writings give importance to these issues or matter in a solution manner or in an improvement manner or in a politically effective manner or in a publicly effective manner. We can understand the language of a journalist public intellectual by taking into account both his contemporary social structure and journalistic writings. Intellectuals may deal with any issue but a public intellectual deal with the issues which are related to the people of his time.

In the second chapter, it discusses Gopabandhu Das as a journalist public intellectual. Public intellectuals generally deal with the contemporary issues. It discusses Gopabandhu Das as a journalist-cum-public intellectual and hence it primarily focuses on his journalistic writings to discuss him. Das mostly wrote on contemporary issues in his journalistic writings. He belongs to the pre-independent time and to understand him as a public intellectual, it discussed his time and society clearly. Gopabandhu Das was not doing any work in national level and he was doing activities only inside Odisha. For this reason, this study took Odisha history of pre-independent time especially the time of Das to evaluate him clearly as a public intellectual.

Most people of Odisha and many from outside Odisha know about *Utkalamani* Gopabandhu Das who was a freedom fighter, social worker, lawyer, head of Odisha Congress, founder of **The Satyabadi** journal, The *Samaja* newspaper, all India vice-president of the Lok Sevak Mandal and the most popular leader of Odisha. As Pritish Acharya mentions in the introduction to **Gopabandhu Chayanika**, Gopabandhu Das was born into an ordinary family. He was eight years younger than Mahatma Gandhi and died twenty years before him and thus his life was short. Even after the bad economic condition of his family, he was able to obtain a B.A degree from **Ravenshaw College, Cuttack** and law degree from **Calcutta University** by his own struggle. His financial conditions were nothing like Gandhi's. He took education as the vehicle to change and develop society. He had even started a school. In spreading education, he got the help of four scholars namely **Nilakantha Das**, **Godabarisa Mishra**, **Acharya Harihara Das** and **Krupasindhu Mishra**. They all together established **Satyabadi Banabidyalaya (Satyabadi School)**. All were educated scholars. Gopabandhu Das along with these four scholars known as the **Panchasakha ofOdisha (five friends of Odisha)**. Many people helped economically and supported to run Satyabadi Banabidyalaya. Like many social workers helped Gandhi to succeed in his leading movements similarly many social workers helped Gopabandhu in Odisha. Gopabandhu used to help poor and flood affected people of **Odisha**. Though he had selected a little geographical place to do service for people but he was not a nationalist in belief but was a universalist. He wrote many journalistic writings in **Odia** language and on issues of **Odisha**. He was using journalistic writings to achieve more success in his social work. He did not only social works but also was giving knowledge on real world to his **Odisha** public through his journalistic writings. He knew the importance of newspaper and journalistic writings and used properly to cover a large number of people within short time.

In third chapter, it shed light on **Surendra Mohanty** (1922-1990) as a journalist and public intellectual. He is a professional writer and secondly a politician. He wrote many valuable literary works in his life-time. He got many awards for his contributions to literature such as **Padma Shree Award, Odisha Sahitya Academy Award, Sarala Award, Central SahityaAcademy Award** etc. His journalist career gave him opportunity to enter into politics. But his politics career helped him to deal with political issues and corruption issues in his journalistic writings. Though he spent his twenty-five years of life in pre-independent India but he spent his rest forty-three years in post-independent India. He started his journalist career just three years before the freedom of India. He started his journal writings in **New Odisha** *journal* which writing was a review of the drama **Atibadi Jagannath Das**and by that he got positive response from the readers. Then he worked as a proof reader in **New Odisha**journal. By the profession of proof reading, he got a good knowledge on journal writings. From **The Observer**journal (which was the only English journal at that time) he started his real journalist career by writing articles. He struggled so much for his career. He spent most of his life-time as a journalist. From Odia journal **Janata**he got the most popularity as a journalist in Odisha. For his satiric writings against government, he was jailed and his publishing house was destroyed by police. But he did not stop his journalistic writings and again started that **Janata**journal by facing many problems. He as a journalist belongs to the post-independent time. We can find that his journalistic writings are belongs to the post-independent time. Surendra Mohanty deals with many contemporary problems of his time. As a litterateur, he gives more emphasis to the development of literature and he writes many journalistic writings on this. In chapter III, it briefly discusses the situation of the society in post-independent Odisha. In post-independence time education system developed but not entirely free of problems. Surendra Mohanty deals with many such issues in his journalistic writings. Corruption is one of the major problems in post-independent Odisha and Surendra Mohanty deals with this issue also in his journalistic writings. It discusses those problems briefly to which Surendra Mohanty deals in his journalistic writings. Corruption, exploitation, lack of good education system, starvation of poor people, lack of employment for people etc., many problems we can see in the time of Surendra Mohanty in Odisha.

Public, Public Sphere and Public Intellectuals

In this chapter, it is wished to delineate concepts like Public, public sphere and public intellectual by tracing their history in the West, and how these notions were used and transformed in colonial and postcolonial context. Keeping the example of the Indian state Odisha in mind, it is argued that the advent of print in Odisha was responsible for a creation of a public sphere whose primary concerns were nationalistic in their spirit. Consequently, the idea of a public intellectual was essentially tied to participation in the nationalist movement.

I

The term 'public', 'public sphere' and 'public intellectual' are connected with each other and to understand their relation we must understand these terms individually. I would like to start a discussion on the concept of 'public'. The word or term 'public' comes from **Latin 'publicus'** and the equivalent of this word in English is '**populace**' which means population in association with some matter of common interest. **Cambridge Dictionary** defines the term as, "relating to or involving people in general rather than being limited to a particular group of people:

Public opinion (= the opinions of most people) has turned against him. Is it really in the public interest (= useful to people) to publish this information? We need to increase public awareness of the disease." In **Oxford English Dictionary** it means, "of, concerning or for the use of the people as a whole." And as a noun it means, "members of the community in general." In **Mariam Webster Dictionary** it is defined as, "of, relating to, or affecting all the people or the whole area of a nation or state." People of a society can be called the public and on the other hand a group of people who are counted differently for their identification are also called public. In politics public means group of individuals directly or indirectly related with politics or who can vote to elect government. . . In a movement, public means people who participate in that movement... Above all public means people who show certain similarities in a society or in an area. There is a relation between the notion 'public' and 'republic'. I have already discussed the term 'public'. The word '**Republic**' was coined by **Plato** in his book *Republic*. He sought inspiration from the term 'justice' used by his teacher **Socrates. Oxford Dictionary** defines the word republic as, "A state in which supreme power is held by the people and their elected representatives, and which has an elected or nominated president rather than a monarch." From these definitions we can infer that the term is mostly a political term which refers to a system where people of a certain area choose their leader to govern that society systematically. In other words, we can say that people of a state or area are entitled to participate in a political process. The notion public and republic are, therefore, interlinked. The idea of public, here means a group of people who share a common cause or have been brought together for a common purpose. However, members of what was called a public were not deeply engaged in interaction with each other, and in any case the Platonic concept of republic included a privileged few. Even though the very term republic in itself implied a participatory form of governance and not necessarily a monarchy, the aims of such a model of governance were actualized only centuries later. The weakening of monarchy, expansion of mercantile enterprise and emergence of civic humanism which happened centuries later, accounted for the rise of a more politically active public. The term 'public sphere' was coined by the German philosopher **Jurgen Habermas**. In a society, there are many problems available and people of that society come together and discuss those problems which discussion might be on politics and other things such as literature, economy etc., and these discussions called public sphere. In other words, to say that the rational discussions of people on certain topics is called public sphere. According to Habermas, those discussions should be secular, rational and valuable. In the book *Habermas*, Andrew Edgar makes the point of Habermas clear that,

These social institutions that allow for open and rational debate between citizens in order to form public opinion. The debate can be conducted face to face or through exchanges of letters and other written communications, and may be mediated by journals, newspapers and electronic forms of communication. Ideally public sphere should be open to all, and agreement should be secured through the force of better argument, rather than through any exercise or threat of physical force. (Edgar Andrew, 124)

For public sphere, freedom is a necessary tool because without freedom it is difficult to discuss anything against injustices of the society or the state. Public sphere finds it hard to thrive under dictatorship. The discussion of people can also happen through indirect talk (discussions through letters or through other written and spoken form). Technological innovation and advancement especially printing press helped people to acquire knowledge which in turn became the major reason why people started having rational discussions. Because of the innovation of printing press, it was possible to publish pamphlets, books, journals, newspapers etc. The facility of printing paper or books or newspaper helped people to know the world and to hold discussions in a rational manner. In Habermas' formulation, discussions which are rational but not secular, would not form a part of the public sphere. Discussions on certain religion would not be associated with public sphere. There are many religions and for that we can see many religious communities. Every religion has some distinct discussions. But we cannot ignore the role of religion in public sphere. Habermas firstly follows the secular notion to define public sphere but later he also accepts the role of religion in public sphere. He accepts the role of religion in the formation of political public sphere. He accepts the role of morality which religion gives to people and which morality help to improve society. We may not accept a religious discussion as public sphere but it has also part in society making and changing like public sphere. Hence there is a big confusion we can find that whether we can call religious discussion a public sphere. We can see a difference between religious discussion and public discussion. There are different religious discussions of different religion community we can find in a secular society. There are many situations and conditions that help in create a public sphere tradition. The tradition of public discussion is not new but the manner of rational and secular discussions come after the innovation of printing machine which helped to spread knowledge and helped to educate people. Apart from the printing, there were some other factors which helped to bring public sphere tradition in Europe which Habermas discussed in his book *Structural Transformation of the Public Sphere*. From bourgeois public sphere, the tradition of public sphere started in Europe. The tradition of letter-writing of bourgeois and then to read those letters in front of people by which people enjoyed those writings and were discussing those writings and this was one of the reasons which paved way for public discussion and creation of public sphere. What Habermas said that letter writing and its development was the reason for starting the tradition of novel writing in Europe. Through literature a reading tradition developed and then of discussion and reaction. People met at salon, coffee house etc, and their discussion would give shape to public sphere. Through these mediums, political public sphere came into existence. Journalism made this public sphere more important and more valuable. Then establishment of welfare country in early 20th century brought a type of effective public sphere in Europe. And due to change of time the notion of public sphere changed in Europe.

There is a relation between public and public sphere. As I discussed above that public sphere is a discussion of people or public for various reason and the public means a group of people who are connected for some common reason. We can understand that the structure of public comes first in an area and after the possible structure of public the concept 'public sphere' became possible. Without the structure of public, a public discussion or public sphere is not possible. Now I will make it clear through an example. Suppose in an area there are seven people living but all are living so distance from each other and nobody have any relation with each other and they are living under no society system. But after some year their population increase and they started to depend in each other for food and business. After some year they become a society and except food and business people of that area come into contact for various issues of their society and from those contact the 'public' notion created (people are connected for some common reason and we call those people public who come under some similar point or reason) and after they come into contact with each other they also started discussion together for various problems and issues in their society and from those discussion public sphere concept become possible.

II

Like European countries, in Odisha also there are many reasons for the emergence of public sphere tradition. There are some similarities with Europe which accounted for the public sphere and these include establishment of printing press, circulation of books and newspapers, and the reading public. But the history and other social situations of Odisha are different from those of Europe. Odisha had been ruled by many foreign states and countries before 1947. From 1434 A.D to 1541 A.D **Odisha** had been ruled by **The Suryavanshi**, from 1568 A.D to 1591 A.D **Odisha** ruled by **Afghan**, from 1592 A.D to 1751 A.D **Odisha** ruled by **Mughal**, from 1751 A.D to 1803 A.D **Odisha** was under the **Marathas**. British took over Odisha in 1803 and ruled till 1947, the year when India became independent. Having been ruled by different people at different points in time, Odisha's culture was influenced by diverse sources. It is not necessary to discuss total ancient history to understand the tradition of public sphere and public intellectual. It is enough to discuss from 19th century onward to understand these issues. British government neglected and exploited Odisha and gave importance to the education only for their own benefit to create some job for their business and to do more business through the help of educated people. In different part of **Odisha**, different languages such as Persian, Bengali, Hindi, Telugu, Tamil etc. were established as official languages and in this way British government neglected and insulted **Odia** language. But many intellectuals of **Odisha** saved **Odisha** from this problem. Due to the efforts made by Fakirmohan Senapati, Madhusudan Rao, Radhanath Ray, Madhusudan Das, Gopabandhu Das and many other intellectuals, Odisha became a separate province in 1936 on linguistic basis. It was the first province along with Sindh to have been accorded such a status. Like in many European countries, in Odisha too the public sphere at large and particularly the public intellectuals essayed a pivotal role. Before printing machine came to **Odisha**, there was a hand-written newspaper called *Kujbar Patra* edited by Sadhu Sunder Das which was being circulated during the year 1769 but it was practically impossible to distribute hand written newspaper everywhere and that paper could reach some central areas only. In 1837, Christian Missionaries established a printing press in Cuttack which was known as 'The Cuttack Mission Press'. As we know that the introduction of printing machine brought a revolution in spread of education and knowledge which in turn, were responsible for the emergence of an intelligensia and also a conducive environment to nurture them. In 1866, The *Na-anka* or the nine-digit famine hit Odisha and consequently more than one million people lost their lives. The British Government showed utter negligence in their handling of the situation. At that time printing facility was available in Odisha and there was serious need of newspaper to improve various situations such as famine and flood situation, food problems, information problem for poor especially for poor people, improvemental knowledges for poor people etc. Finally, a periodical named **The Utkal Dipika** was started by Gouri Shankar Ray in 1866 which remained in circulation till 1934. From 1866, serially many newspapers started in **Odisha** which include: **Sambad Vahika** in 1868 started by Fakir Mohan Senapati and Govind Patnaik, **Utkal Putra** in 1873 started by Pyari Mohan Acharya, **Samskaraka**in 1883 started by Chaturbhuj Patnaik, etc. In this way periodicals and newspapers continually strove for the development of the region. Before establishment of newspaper, especially before the 1860s we do not find any social group that held public discussions in a both rational and secular manner. There were discussions happening on religion, on spirituality, on morality, on soul purification etc., and Scholar like Jagannath Das was campaigning on religious and spiritual matter. There were gatherings of people, movements, revolts, rebellions happening and some of the examples are **Paika Rebellion** against British Government in 1804, **Prolonged Revolt** in 1827, **Keonjhar *Meli*** in 1866 etc. There were rare discussions happening on any physical reformation or physical problems of people or societies rather than spiritual and moral and we cannot call those discussions as public sphere without rational, secular, and valuable discussion. We also can see that a tradition of public discussion by different Sabha and Samiti (social groups and committees) started after the establishment of printing press and after the tradition of intellectuals and journalist intellectuals. Different type of public sphere was coming out from many different Sabha and Samiti and some of those are 'All India Khadi Board', 'District Congress Committee', 'Utkal Provincial Congress Committee', 'Utkal Swarajya Siksha Committee', 'Utkal Union Conference'. In these social institutions a large number of public discussions were happening and those were the public sphere which affected British Government. For many social actions and social movements or revolt, decisions were taken from those social institutions. Newspapers were working for people and society and those newspapers had the major role to create public sphere at that time. Because modern press established in Odisha, many intellectuals came into existence and many started use newspapers and magazines to create a reformation in society, to awake people and to create public sphere. Great intellectuals like Fakir Mohan Senapati, Madhusudan Das, Gouri Shankar Roy, Radhanath Roy, Gopabandhu Das, Nilakantha Das, Godabarish Mishra, Biswanath Das etc, were the great leader of different movement and reformation in Odisha. All these scholars used newspaper and magazine to communicate their thought with people. Their writings were on literature, social and political issues. Because of modern press and intellectual the tradition of public sphere got large shape. Both newspapers and public intellectuals played a big role for social reformation in Odisha. Journalist public intellectuals like Gopabandhu Das used newspaper and magazine successfully. Because of his journalistic writings, large number of people started to join in meetings, in discussions, in movements, in Congress works etc. In

Many of his journalistic writings he deals with the major problems of the Odisha at that time such as starvation of poor people, famine, lack of work, lack of education etc. Not only Gopabandhu Das but also many other intellectuals and journalist public intellectuals deal with these problems in their writings. Many intellectuals like Gopabandhu Das were doing both direct service for people and through their writings. At that time mostly, public sphere was leading by intellectuals in different meetings and social institutions. In public discussions leaders were chosen and then people were presenting different problems and suggested solutions and finally the leaders were deciding and presenting their thoughts and often solutions in those meetings. In many journalistic writings, Gopabandhu Das appealed people to join in those meetings. Gopabandhu Das used to go to attained many public meetings and discussions and people at that time took him as the leader of Odisha. Both by his direct speech to people and by his journalistic writings he worked as a public intellectual and as a journalist public intellectual. At that time involvement of people in movements was one of the major problems and for which he wrote some journalistic writings such as '**Mukha Na Phitile Dukha Jae Nanhi**', '**Sinha Bhumi Bhaiku Niras Kara Nanhi**', '**Gadajatare Prajameli**', '**Congress' Work is National Work**' etc. To give information on famine suffering people and to get help from people and to encourage helping people he wrote journalistic writings such as '**Flood and Famine in Odisha**', '**Everywhere Famine**', '**Description of Direct Flood Experience**' etc. For unity of Odia language area, he wrote '**Making of State on Language Basis**', '**Gandhiji Wants Special Odisha**', '**Special Odisha State**' etc. For education he wrote many journalistic writings such as '**Higher Education by**

Vernacular Language', 'Education and Agriculture', 'Labour and Education', 'Not to Give Child Vernacular Education is to Kill Them', 'Education and Peace', 'Making of Students' Life' etc. Gopabandhu Dealt with almost all major problems of his time in his journalistic writings. He properly used the medium of newspaper to improve social conditions. Not only Gopabandhu Das but also many intellectuals used newspaper as the medium of social reformation.

There is deep connection between public intellectual and public sphere. As we know that public sphere tradition come to Odisha after the establishment printing press. Because of printing machine facility, education and knowledge spread through the form of printing press, books, magazines, newspapers etc. Because of this technology, it was possible to reach knowledge to people. Availability of press, books, newspapers increase the rational power, world knowledge, moral knowledge etc., in people. But we cannot claim that intellectuals are created after the facility of different books, press and other forms of knowledge. Intellectuals can observe reality, other matters by their thought and they can also give solutions by their thought power. But after the facility of different form of knowledge, it affects the thought and visual process of intellectuals. We can find relations between public sphere and public intellectuals after the facility of different form of knowledge. These knowledge forms are the bridge between public sphere and public intellectuals. Because of available of knowledge form, many people could gain knowledge and many of them could function as intellectual and many of them could function for people as intellectual. Because of knowledge facility many intellectuals could deal more properly in public or in newspapers. Because those public intellectuals shared their thought through newspaper, common people could get the thoughts of intellectuals and those thoughts helped people to think from rational and practical point of view. Available of different thoughts of intellectuals in newspapers helped people think and discuss in a valuable manner and also helped to create public sphere. In this way, we can find relations between public intellectuals and public sphere. Intellectuals like Gouri Shankar Ray, Bichitrananda Das, Fakir Mohan Senapati, Madhusudan Das, Gopabandhu Das got the help of different form of knowledge to educate themselves and through the medium of newspapers and magazines, they communicated their thoughts with people which helped to create different public sphere in Odisha.

Due to changing situations and conditions, the notion of public sphere and public intellectual have been changing. Above discussed matters are from pre-independence time. In 1947, India got freedom and many conditions and situations had changed. In post-independent era, people enjoyed the freedom and enjoyed the right to choose their own government. Harekrushna Mahatab became the first chief-minister of Odisha in 27 may 1947. Like other states of India, in Odisha also democratic system of government started. By the effort of Sardar Ballabh Bhai Patel, different scatter area mixed in Odisha and became one Odisha state. People got freedom and started to do work freely. After freedom, people of Odisha started enjoying their culture. Because people gained the power of vote, government became conscious towards people. But freedom can never stop different social problems. Even after the freedom of India and Odisha, people would not stop raising voice against government due to various social problems. Public gatherings and public discussions continued after freedom also. According to Surendra Mohanty's auto-biography in the section 'Union of Gadjat and Separation of Sadheikala-Kharasuan' he wrote on the incident which happened January 1, 1948. Tribal people of Kharasuan started to gather and oppose the decision of Kharasuan king without any information to them. Kharasuan king agreed to mix his state in Odisha and because of this reason tribal people started gathering visit to meet the king but Kharasuan police did not agree to let them meet but those people and like Jalibanawalabag incident here also more than 700 people lost their lives. They only wanted to meet their king but without any strong reason those people were killed. After freedom also, people were suffering from many problems. After freedom, corruption is a major issue which also mentioned by Surendra Mohanty in his auto-biography. Government also worked in many areas to solve social problems. **Biju Patnaik** successfully industrialized Rourkela area to develop economic condition of Odisha. Surendra Mohanty used to call **Biju Patnaik** as industrial man because of his effort.

In post-independent time also the tradition of public discussion, public sphere and public intellectual continued. In post-independent time newspaper and magazine got more freedom but here is also we can find problems. Because of his satire on Congress government in his *Janata* magazine, Surendra Mohanty was punished and sent to jail by Odisha government. Hence, from pre-independent time to till now the tradition public sphere have been part of our society. For different social problems, people with gathering were discussing in a rational and secular manner to effect government and to change the situation. As the result of these public sphere, many times big movements, protests, revolts against government come out. For different problems in society, different public intellectuals and different newspapers worked for successful public sphere making. Journals and newspapers successfully reach to a vast number of public and for this reason many public intellectuals used this medium to discuss on social issues and problems in a rational manner. Because of successful use of newspaper and journals by intellectuals, public sphere tradition gradually became the large part of Odisha and of course in India.

Surendra Mohanty, who was the part of both pre-independent and post-independent time, wrote many journalistic writings on the post-independent picture of Odisha. Different intellectuals take different topic to discuss and Surendra Mohanty took mostly literature issues in his journalistic writings to discuss. In most of his writings he shows the defects in literature and in many he gives his opinions on issues and in many he also writes on solutions to many problems. He also writes on the corruption of his contemporary government. After the freedom of India, in the first general Lok Sabha election Jawaharlal Nehru (first prime minister of India) came to Balangir district for election campaign and Surendra Mohanty wrote a khola chithhi (open letter) to Jawaharlal Nehru in which letter he wrote on the corruptions of Congress government which letter got published in the same day of Nehru's speech at Balangir. Because of that article Nehru faced many bad reactions from people in his election campaign. That article spread everywhere in Odisha which created a type of public discussion at that time. This is a proper example that how a journalistic writing can create a public reaction within a short time. Even Surendra Mohanty got threats from many people. In his auto-biography, he wrote on how Nehru got angry for this writing in the section title 'Open Letter to Pandit Jawaharlal Nehru and the First General Election'. Many journalists public intellectuals do such type of writings to draw attention of the government during election time. It is the power of newspaper and intellectual journalists who can Shape public opinion and make it possible for discussions to take place, through their journalistic writings.

All the three concepts that is public, public sphere and public intellectual are inter-related. If we see the notion public deeply then we can find that public sphere also comes after the existence of social structure. Because of society structure, people live in certain area and came into contact with each other by which the notion of public (means a group of people with some common reason came into contact) became possible. I discussed above the relation among public, public sphere and public intellectuals. The connotations of these three terms have been changing from time to time. Due to social system these three systems exist. We can understand this if we compare Gopabandhu Das' political milieu and Surendra Mohanty'. Gopabandhu Das lived between 1877 to 1928 whereas Surendra Mohanty lived from1922 to 1990. Time of Gopabandhu Das was full of problems and struggles. Poverty problem, famine and flood problem, language problem, disease problems, death of people problem, lack of involvement of people in movements and other social work and freedom problem are many major problems we can see in his time and the journalistic writings of Gopabandhu Das are clear evident of those problems. On the other hand, during Surendra Mohanty these problems reduced to a better situation. During his time the access of newspaper increased, involvement of people in different social work and movements was also increased, Odia language problem got solved, Unity of Odia language area problem got solved, and freedom problem mostly solved after independence. Surendra Mohanty enjoyed most of his life time in an independent India. The problems during Surendra Mohanty's times were in many ways different from the time of Gopabandhu Das. In many of his journalistic writings, Surendra Mohanty deals with the problems of development, corruption, standardization of education, literature etc. Because social structure changed, the dealing issues of different intellectuals also changed. Public also changed due to change of social structure. During the time of Gopabandhu Das the discussion of non-cooperation to British government, discussion on famine, discussions on starvation of poor, discussions on income/employment and work, discussions on education often took place in different sabhas and samitis. The public sphere had changed visibly in the time of Surendra Mohanty when most discussions were on parties and politics, on corruption of government, on education development, on government policies for poor people, on industrial development, on literature development happening in different social institutions and in different newspapers and magazines. After independence, people and journals got more freedom and a type of open discussion against different social evil started. During the time of Gopabandhu Das, journalist was not a lucrative profession and people from other profession were writing journalistic writings. But in the time of Surendra Mohanty, journalism became a special profession and by which many journalists could work only for journal which I discuss in third chapter. In this way we can see how time to time situations and then public sphere and the very idea of public intellectual have been changing.

Journalist as Public Intellectual in Pre-Independent Time: The Case of Gopabandhu Das

The notion of 'public intellectual' is not fixed and its defining characteristics depend on its contemporary society, political climate and prevailing discourses on public figures and the role of the intelligentsia. Public intellectuals deal or are often expected to deal directly with issues concerning the public, and communicate their ideas with people. Public intellectuals may or may not be equated always with academic intellectuals. In pre-independent India for instance leaders who more or less functioned like public intellectuals, like Gandhi, Nehru et.al. were not university professors or teachers of any kind. Even in present day India, many of the public intellectuals like Ramachandra Guha and Arundhati Roy are not institutionally affiliated scholars. Academic intellectuals are generally educationists who write, lecture and are sometimes involved in policy-making activities and projects; whereas public intellectuals are more directly involved with the public in the sense that the primary target of their intellectual exercise is the (reading) public. As is often seen, public intellectuals engage in contemporary debates. There are many world-wide discussions happening on 'intellectuals' and 'public intellectuals.' There are also many discussions centering on the roles and characteristics of public intellectuals. In modern times it is a part of broad discussion. Many writers have written on public intellectual in the national context like Romila Thapar whose book *The Public Intellectual in India* (2016) offers a discussion on the idea of public intellectual in India. In my dissertation, I aim to shed light specifically on the idea of journalists as public intellectuals rather than the all aspects of public intellectuals. In this chapter, I will explore the journalistic writings of Gopabandhu Das (1877-1928), the context of Odisha, to examine his role as a public intellectual.

Before understanding Gopabandhu Das as public intellectual, we should discuss the situations and conditions of his time i.e., the pre-in dependent times and the movement for formation of a separate Odia speaking state. As I discussed above that public-intellectuals are deeply related with the social structure of their times. Gopabandhu Das lived for fifty years, 1877 to 1928. During this time the British had already been ruling India and

Odisha. They had in fact occupied Odisha in 1803. They first came to Odisha during 1633 for purposes of trade after seeking permission from the Mughal administrator. After the battle of Plassey in 1757 and Buxar in 1764, The British started to capture a vast area of India. Diplomacy could not help the British in acquiring Odisha. Lord Wellesley, the aggressive Governor-General, decided to acquire Odisha by force. In 1803, the Deogan treaty was signed by which Maratha rule ended and British rule started in Odisha. The British acquired administrative powers and started exploiting the people of Odisha by using their power and diplomacy. They neglected Odisha and caused great harm to the prosperous economical condition of Odisha. They divided Odisha into different divisions and tagged them with different cultural and political units. Cuttack, Puri and Balasore were attached to the Bengal Presidency; Sambalpur was ruled by central provinces, Ganjam, Phulbani and Koraput were placed under the Madras Presidency. Beside these, there were twenty-six feudatory states ruled by local kings but were supervised by the British. In this way Odisha had completely lost its unity and identity under British rule. Another big problem created by British government was language problem. British government showed utter negligence towards Odia language and established Persian, Bengali, Hindi, Telugu, Tamil etc., in different parts of Odisha as the official language. But **Odisha** people were not silent against the exploitation of the British. They mounted strong opposition against the Britishers. We can see the different movements in the pre-independent history of Odisha. Britishers were collecting revenue from Odisha people in a brutal manner. They were badly exploiting even the poor people. Many kings and other people waged wars, organized revolts, movements but those were brutally suppressed. In 1804 **Jai Rajguru** declared war against the British but this was ineffective and Jai Rajguru was executed. During 1817 a dangerous rebellion broke out and spread in Khurdha and nearby areas. The rebellion took big shape which is known as **Paika Rebellion. Bakshi Jagabandhu** was the leader of this Paika Rebellion movement. People attacked police stations, and treasuries, destroyed many British properties. This rebellion reached Puri and caused similar problems for the British. Taking inspiration from this movement, many other movements started against British rule. Prolonged revolts in Sambalpur were led by Surendra Sai between 1827-64, in Angul in 1848, in Bamanaghati in 1866, in Keonjhar in 1866 and 1891-93. These movements compelled the British government to change some of their policies. But the situation in Odisha got worse. Under British rule, the economic situation was declining continually. British government was totally neglecting Odisha. During 1866, a dangerous famine i.e., **Na-Anka** famine struck Odisha, and here, the British government showed complete negligence. In this famine more than one million people lost their lives. This was the situation which opened the eyes of many and provoked many intellectuals to come forward and improve the existing conditions in Odisha. Historian Pritish Acharya observes:

The intelligentsia looked afresh at the nature of British rule and linked it with the underdevelopment of the state. The tragedy was largely attributed to the government's unwise policy. The inadequate relief and the state's laissez policy did little to check the price rise and pushed the poor people to starvation. The native officials being mostly "outsiders" (non-Oriyas), apparently misled the administration. The intelligentsia complained that this aggravated the crises. Following the famine, the intellectuals began to address both the administration as well as people. Such efforts at establishing a two-way link between the authorities and the people ushered in the process of mobilization of people, and of the nation-making in Orissa. The year 1866, thus, became a turning point in the modern history of the state. (Acharya Pritish 5)

The process of exploitation continued in the time of Gopabandhu Das also. During the time of Gopabandhu Das, Odisha was suffering from many problems and some major problems were poverty, starvation of poor people, famine, crisis in education system, the difficulty of uniting Odia-speaking tracts, protecting Odia language from continuous onslaught by Bengali intellectuals who were bent on effacing the language from all forms of public discourse. These problems were not new to the time of Gopabandhu Das. Many intellectuals and public figures had made effort to better these situations of Odisha. These included figures like Gouri Shankar Ray, Madhusudan Das, Fakir Mohan Senapati, Radhanath Ray, Bichitrananda Das et al. The Na-Anka famine of 1866 had caused great intellectual awakening. After this tragedy, intellectuals first focused on the ignorance of common people. To solve that problem intellectuals started to establish newspaper and magazines. These intellectuals were instrumental in expansion of knowledge. Except intellectuals, many princes and zamindars offered financial help in establishing educational institutions and in improving the state of affairs of education, at large. In 1870s, Pyari Mohan Acharya, a renowned historian, started Cuttack Academy which became a high school in 1879. Madhusudan Rao (1853-1912), the famous poet, taught at a government school and wrote journalistic articles and ran a journal title *Shikshabandhu* for motivating teachers. The first Odia primer is attributed to his name. Fakir Mohan Senapati (1843-1918), a great writer, started a high school at Remuna in Balasore, Radhanath Ray played an important role in the spread of education in Odisha. Intellectuals also groomed good students. In 1903, Utkal Samilani was founded in which many discussions took place and many an important decision were taken to develop the condition of education in Odisha (especially in gadajat areas). During his time, Gopabandhu Das took the efforts made for educational development to its next level. Intellectuals before Gopabandhu Das ran newspapers for social reformation in Odisha. Gouri Shankar Ray and Bichitrananda Das started the *Utkal Dipika* in 1866, Fakir Mohan Senapati and Govind Patnaik started *Sambad Vahika* in 1868, Pyari Mohan Acharya started the *Utkal Putra* in 1873, Chaturbhuj Patnaik started the *Samskaraka* in 1883 etc. Gopabandhu Das also established a journal called *The Satyabadi* and a newspaper, *The Samaja* but he followed his own principles to improve the existing conditions in the society. Gopabandhu Das did not deal with the social evils and superstitions and regressive ideas in his journalistic writings but he dealt with educational development which was, for him, the tool to get rid of social evils and regressive practices.

During the time of Gopabandhu Das, the situations of poor people was grim. Death of people by starvation was a regular problem. Health was also a major issue and the mortality rate was fairly high. Lack of employment for people was one of the major problems at that time. Though the intellectual predecessors of Gopabandhu had worked hard enough to improve the lot of the Odias, much improvement was still needed. Next, we will focus on the topic of public intellectuals vis-à-vis the journalistic writings of Gopabandhu Das and how he dealt with those social issues through his writings.

Newspapers and society are deeply related to each other and in this way journalists and society also share a deep relation. From 17th century onwards, newspapers have been a medium of information. In modern world, newspapers became a regular part of public life. It is not only a medium of information but also a medium of social change and social development. By the medium of newspapers, many journalists, many intellectuals and many public intellectuals do beneficial service for people and society by their journalistic writings. It is mostly a successful medium to communicate with people. Intellectuals who write for development of society and with the intention of bringing improvement, can be called public intellectuals. Such types of journalists and intellectuals are the men of education and wisdom and they write journalistic pieces in connection with contemporary society and people. Their writings become their medium of rendering service to people. A newspaper not only deals with political information but also deals with every type of social reality and issues. One public intellectual may write on health issues to raise awareness among people. One may write on literature to revive its greatness; one may write on religion to infuse spirituality among people. The two public intellectuals whose writings I discuss in my book, pursued different professions and belonged to different era. Both Gopabandhu Das and Surendra Mohanty covered a large readership in Odisha. Both dealt with their contemporary issues and problems. It is imperative to explore their journalistic writings in order to understand their status as leading public intellectual of their times. At the same time, it is equally important to remember that while the former had an activist' orientation, the latter was known primarily as a litterateur and columnist.

In order to proceed further into the discussion, it is important to reemphasize the factors which accord the status of intellectuals to journalist. Antonio Gramsci contends 'all men are intellectuals' but he also argues that only few people from society can function as intellectuals (Gramsci). Social structures play decisive roles in shaping their intellectual milieu and therefore influence their intellectuals in complex ways. Steve Jones remarks,

So, while art has been an intellectual activity for some centuries, until the twentieth century design was relegated to position of practical knowledge (both would now be seen as intellectual activity with appropriate certification). Cooking and eating have generally seen as mundane and practical activities, but they now have an expanded category of culinary intellectuals- TV chefs, journalists, restaurateurs, nutritionists and so on-who mediate between food producers and the public, confirming the rightness or otherwise of a person's taste choices. (Jones 82)

Although Jones seems to have a contemporary western society in mind, the importance of his argument lies in the fact that recognition as a public intellectual rest on participation in matters which are of interest to the public. The other important point to be gleaned from Jones' exposition is that the emergence of a public intellectual goes in a parallel fashion with the development of specialized fields of knowledge. The shaping up of public intellectuals is therefore incumbent on certain discursive formations. In the context of Gopabandhu Das, the discursive formations pertain to the nationalist movement in general and the call for creation of a separate Odia speaking province in particular. In the case of the other journalist-cum-public intellectual, Surendra Mohanty (who I shall discuss at lengths in the subsequent chapter) the discursive practices had to do with the professionalization of journalism in India and the niche that was carved out for public figures on the newspapers.

Gopabandhu Das started his own journal with some friends. It was a literary journal and was named **The Satyabadi**. He also started *The Samaja* to communicate with people of his time and in *The Satyabadi*, **The Samaja**, and in some other newspapers he wrote journalistic writings to improve and change the situation of the society of his time. In the book *National Movement and Politics in Orissa*,Pritish Acharya cites the reason behind establishment of newspapers and also gives clear picture of movements and politics of Odisha from 1920 to 1929.Because of many problems, intelligentsia of Odisha felt to give information to people for improvement of situations and for this reason, the Odia intelligentsia started to establish newspaper in Odia. Acharya reasons,

As a way out, the intelligentsia founded the modern press. Following the famine, Gourishankar Ray started the Utkal Deepika, the first Oriya weekly, in 1866, making it possible for Orissa-related issues to be publicly debated. Similarly, Fakir Mohan and Govind Patnaik brought out the *Sambad Vahika* (1868) from Balasore, Pyari Mohan Acharya, the *Utkal Putra* (1873) and Chaturbhuj Patnaik, the *Samskaraka* (1883), from Cuttack. The number of newspapers and journals, which stood at only four in 1871, increased to nine by 1879, 19 by 1889 and 34 by 1900." (Acharya 9).

He further states,

Newspapers at the time were neither business enterprises nor were their editors and journalists professionals. Journalism was seen as a means nationalist struggle rather than a lucrative profession. They were, in general, published as a public service and financed as objects of philanthropy. (9)

Gopabandhu Das felt the need for a newspaper for public service and for improvement of people's condition which can be understood from his 1919 speech at the commemoration of the fourth year of the Utkal Samilini. In this speech he calls for a type of newspaper which would be devoted to issues like health, education, co-operative committee, agriculture, knowledge on cottage industries (intended for rural people); there would also be foreign news and such type of newspaper would be discussed in the villages where the **Bhagavad Gita**is otherwise discussed. In those days the villages would have a place assigned for public reading of the **Bhagavad Gita**, and Gopabandhu Das wanted to use that space for spread of education and knowledge. The situation of education was very poor, then. There were many newspapers available but he wanted to start his own press. There could be two reasons why Gopabandhu wanted to start a newspaper: one is to extend his social work through newspaper, the other is his desire for a different kind of newspaper. Various editions of *Utkal Dipika* of 1918 and of 1919 are full of advertisements and we can find both English and Odia news. Important events and incidents did find place in the newspaper, but the medium seemed ineffective for society, since they merely carried information without giving any call for public participation or explicitly arousing nationalist sentiments. We can mark clear differences between the writings of Gopabandhu Das and the writings published in *Utkal*

Dipika. He delivered this speech in 1919 where he mentioned his desire for a different kind of newspaper and later in the same year, he started the weekly *The Samaja*. Gopabandhu Das was primarily a social worker and he knew it very well that proper use of a newspaper could improve the miserable situation prevailing in Odisha. His journalistic writings directly deal with public issues. In many of his journalistic writings he directly appeals to the people and read like open letter to the people. We can see that in most of his journalistic writings he tries to awake people, provoke them for taking action and engage in work which are beneficial for society and people.

Most of the journalistic writings of Gopabandhu Das are collected in the book entitled **Gopabandhu Chayanika**. In this book his speech in the fourth year of Utkal Samilani have also been collected. All type of journalistic writings of Gopabandhu Das are divided into eight categories in *Gopabandhu Chayanika* book and these eight categories are the different aspects of his society which he dealt in his journalistic writings. These eight parts are 'State Politics', 'National Politics', 'World Window', 'Social Questions', 'Society, Tradition and Culture', 'Education', 'Consideration of Language and Literature' and 'biographical sketches'. These eight categories present the major issues of his contemporary society and world. Under the 'State Politics' heading, all writings of freedom movement and other problems of Odisha such as disunity of Odia language area, problems of establishment of Odia language, less involvement of Odia people in national movements and in congress etc. are collected. Under the heading 'Nation Politics', we find writings on the nationalist movement, appeal to students, on Mahatma Gandhi, and other writings. Under the 'Window to the World' category, writings on world politics and freedom movements, on politics in Europe and other India and foreign related writings are collected. In 'Social Question' heading, writings on flood and famine problems in Odisha, misery of poor people, and other social problems are collected. Under the 'Society, Tradition and Culture' heading, journal writings on the problems in Odia society and in Odia beliefs, on Odia culture and tradition and other Odia society related articles are collected. Under the 'Education' heading, his journalistic writings on education related articles are collected. Under the 'Consideration of Language and Literature' heading, journalistic writings on prevailing situation of literature in Odisha and other writings on literature are collected. Under the last heading 'Talk on Persons' the writings of some great persons are collected. The eight broad areas discussed above, neatly capture the major issues which Gopabandhu Das' attention and on which he based his journalistic writings. It would be worth the while to note that Gopabandhu's writings meant to bring knowledge of distant lands closer to home. The writings on the nationalist movement, of course, speak of his politics of merging the Odia sub-nationalist movement with the nationalist struggle. But the focus, on international affairs, for instance, could be seen as a way of modernizing knowledge and broadening people's outlook.

While Gopabandhu was politically active, floods and famines were the major problems in Odisha. Flood and famine are not new problems to Odisha. Gouri Shankar Ray and Bichitrananda Das started the first newspaper of Odisha *The Utkal Dipika* in 1866 and during that time of famine of 1866. The first weekly of *The Utkal Dipika* (henceforth UD) started in August 11,1866 and its first report was 'Famine and Deportment of Calcutta

People' in which a famine conditions in different areas of Odisha are reported. In this report, name of the volunteers and name of the affected areas have been mentioned and it provided beneficial information to the people. In the same newspaper (i.e., UD) in September 21,1907, Gopabandhu Das wrote on the same problem under the heading 'Flood and Famine in Odisha'. There are differences between article of Gopabandhu and of UD on this issue. Gopabandhu Das's journalistic writing clearly describes the situation of people and the affected areas. He writes as he shares his own experience. In his writings he admires people who are helpful in a language which could also motivate the rich to lend a helping hand. His language may lack rhetoric, the simplicity of his prose helps in passing his message clearly.

After entry to the village, we saw that not a single home was in good condition. Walls and roofs had collapsed, the whole place had been muddied. Some of the cottages had been totally destroyed. One could still hear the echoes of their agonizing cry. Some old men were heard saying, "we shall not live more", and some others, "it's better to die; how long shall we go on suffering?" they spent five days on the rooftops of their thatched house without any food. After the water receded, they survived on boiled pumpkin leaves. When asked how they had been living, they replied, 'what to do! We have to make do with the water that is available here, by eating arum leaves, pumpkin leaves, plantain leaves we eat and starve on alternate days. (Das209; my trans)

As is clear from the instance cited above, much of Gopabandhu's writings came directly from experience of visiting the flood-affected areas and he tried to make everyone aware of the grim situation by writing in a plain and clear manner. It is obvious that a public intellectual who has direct experience of public life and situations can deal with public issues more effectively. Gopabandhu Das was the kind of public intellectual that by Romila Thapar in her *The Public Intellectual in India* describes in the following terms,

An intellectual, even without being a public intellectual, requires a more than average knowledge in his/her professional specialization and beyond that a familiarity with the context of that knowledge: how did it came about and what are the implications for the people who use that knowledge. To be a technician (or be technically accomplished) in a specialization, however good, is not sufficient. An intellectual perspective requires that the specialized knowledge one possesses should be related to social concern where required and to other branches of knowledge as well. (Thapar 111)

We can apply Thapar's definition on Gopabandhu Das. He belonged to a poor family and during his time the situation of education was very bad. Pritish Acharya remarks that even despite the poor economic condition of his family, he was able to obtain a B.A degree from Ravenshaw College, Cuttack and a Law degree from Calcutta University. He was not only well-educated by degree but was well aware of the socio-economic conditions of his milieu. He wrote many articles on world affairs such as "The Politics of Europe", "The Situations of Indians in Foreign Countries", "India and Australia", "Context of Africa", "After World War" etc. He wrote many articles on matters of public interest and on major social problems. In many of his journalistic writings he offers simple possible solutions to problems confronting the society. During his time illiteracy and inability to read were some of the pressing concerns. Gopabandhu Das offered a solution for this problem by restarting the reading of Bhagavat Gita which was once the reason for large number having the ability to read. Gopabandhu Das suggests,

This *Bhagavat Gita* book should serve as the guiding light of law of our development. Many ancient Bhagavat temples are still in existence in villages, those should be used for raising cultural awareness. This temple should be established where there is no such temple. Given the faith people have in the *Bhagavat Gita*, such efforts are likely to succeed. The halls meant for reading the *Bhagavat Gita* should become the center of village activities and discussions. The place should be used for holding religious discussions, for people to meet and seek advice and for resolving village disputes. The discussion of village welfare, development of agriculture and industry and other social issues should also take place there. (Page-22-23)

As the instance just cited shows, Gopabandhu did not simply act like a university educated academic but as an intellectual who combined the emphasis on dissemination of education with re-formation of religious practices.

Gopabandhu's deep involvement in social work and public service took away much of his time, and that may explain why he wrote in simple language instead of pruning or adding much literary sophistication to it. But lucidity was also his greatest strength. He knew that by journalistic writings he could reach a large readership within short period. In the introduction to *Gopabandhu Chayanika*, Pritish Acharya maintains,

Unlike other professional essayists, Gopabandhu had little time to finetune his journalistic writings. If we look at his busy life, it would seem that it was not possible for him. He was not a professional essayist in the strictest sense of the term. He wrote down normally by taking socio-political contexts as issues. The writings would then be sent immediately for publication. These are important information and his own opinion on the important subject matter in his journal writings. (Page-xxxviii)

Gopabandhu had relinquished his legal profession because of social work and politics. He was the most popular man in Odisha. Yet he kept his profession of writing alive. He wrote many literary pieces (especially poetry) when he was in jail. He wrote during his train journey; he wrote whenever he got any free time. He produced a significant number of works during his short life time of 50 years. In a life that was cut short by illness, he had managed to visit many villages and had met many people. He had a first-hand experience of situations and problems which confronted the ordinary masses. He wrote prolifically on those issues in his journalistic writings.

Due to social problems, not only Gopabandhu Das but also many other intellectuals were doing different social work to improve the situation of the society and to bring reformation. Some intellectuals were working towards spread of education, some for the poor, some for social reformation by press etc. During 1865-66, Na-Anka Durvikhya (Na-Anka famine) happened in Odisha which took the lives of more than one million people. During this tragedy many members of the intelligentsia started to raise voice against the famine policy of British government. As Pritish Acharya notes,

Following the famine, the intellectuals began to address both the administration as well as the people. Such efforts as establishing a two-way link between the authorities and the people ushered in the process of mobilization of the people, and of nation making in Orissa. The year 1866, thus, became a turning point in the modern history of the state. (Acharya Pritish 5)

In 1866 Gouri Shankar Ray started *The Utkal Dipika* which mostly circulated famine and flood related information. The periodical helped people to get helpful information. Later many intellectuals realized the importance of education for people. Many princes and zamindars helped to establish education system in Odisha and one of the great examples was the prince of Mayurbhanj, Ramachandra Bhanjadeo who donated five thousand rupees to the medical school (1875) and to the Cuttack Collage (1868) in 1877. Pyari Mohan Acharya started Cuttack Academy in early 1870s, Madhusudan Rao, a modern poet, started a journal *Shikshabandhu* to motivate teachers, Fakir Mohan, set up a high school at Remuna in Balasore District, Radhanath Ray, a great poet, worked for promotion of education. Many intellectuals started newspaper for social improvement and reformation. Gouri Shankar Ray and Bichitrananda Das started *The Utkal Dipika* in 1866, Fakir Mohan and Govind Patnaik started *Sambad Vahika* in 1868, Pyari Mohan Acharya started *The Utkal Putra* in 1873, Chaturbhuj Patnaik started *Samskaraka* in 1883 etc. And as Pritish Acharya rightly observes, "they were, in general, published as a public service and financed as objects of philanthropy (citation?)." Many intellectuals had essayed pivotal roles in the development of Odisha. However, things did not change significantly. Famine and flood problems, death of many people due to poor health and starvation, lack of food supply, water problems, lack of education, lack of health care system, no works for poor people, problem of Odia language establishment, lack of unity of Odisha people etc. are the major problems during Gopabandhu Das' time. and

We can see these evident both in the journalistic writings of Gopabandhu Das and in his other writings as well. He continued to reach out to the poor to distribute food packets. Since he could not reach a large number of people, he tried to use the medium of newspaper to make up for direct communication.

Language problem was one of the major issues in pre-independent Odisha. Odia language had been neglected by British Govt. in Odisha. In 1895, the chief commissioner declared that Oriya would be replaced by Hindi to facilitate the transfer of officials within the state. Intelligentsia of Odisha started to solve these problems. In his book, *National Movement and Politics in Orissa*, it is clearly said that,

"Fakir Mohan and the amlas of Balasore held meetings and sent against the possible abortion of Oriya from schools. As lack of textbooks in Oria was cited as a reason for abolishing the language, the intellectuals set out to write textbooks to prove the worth of their language as well as to meet the needs of school education. Madhusudan Rao wrote the *BarnoObodh*, a primer on alphabets, while Fakir Mohan wrote a mathematics primer, *Ankamala*. Gangadhar Meher, a great poet himself, translated a few Hindi poems for primary classes. Radhanath wrote books on all subjects, from geography to mathematics, for primary school students. Bichhad Charan and Gouri Shankar Ray also wrote textbooks to help overcome the shortage." (Page-16)

Other intellectuals wrote books on Odisha. Pyari Mohan acharya wrote **Odishara Itihas**(1991), Gopal Chandra Acharya wrote *Sri Jagannath O Chaitanya*, Jitendra M. Singh wrote the *Odisha Chitra* and Fakir Mohan wrote the *Bharat Itihas* with added emphasis on Odisha. All these intelligentsia made effort to glorify Odisha and Odia language. Gopabandhu Das also made efforts to glorify Odia language. Different intellectuals made efforts in different directions. He established **Satyabadi Bakul Bana Bidyalaya** school in 1909 in Sakhigopala near Puri. The school followed the gurukula system of education and later became high school and subsequently became a national school in 1921. To educate people of Odisha, he launched a monthly literary magazine title *Satyabadi* in 1913. Then in 1919 he started the weekly newspaper *The Samaja* which was totally devoted to society and people of Odisha. Pritish Acharya writes on the contributions of Satyabadi group to Odisha:

It was a school for developing an alternative model of education, a training center for nationalist politics, a sort of nationalist media house, which brought out two journals. The monthly *The Satyavadi* was dedicated to literature and *The Samaja* to socio-political issues.

Satyavadi, [the place from which the journal had taken its name], became a main relief center at that time of floods and other calamities. It was the brainchild of Gopabandhu Das and his young nationalist friends such as Nilakantha Das, Godabarish Mishra, Harihar Das and Anant Mishra. Popularly known as the *Panchasakha* (five friends), this highly educated group had opted for community work as their mission and formed the core of moderate nationalists in the state." (Acharya Pritish 39)

In *The Satyabadi* he wrote an article titled "Higher Education by the Help of Vernacular Language" in which he proposes how vernacular language is important and valuable for the purpose of education. Here he gives examples of how vernacular language can be instrumental in ushering in development. He says that, "Premises of higher education will grow by vernacular education. After university education, educated students will have enough energy and vim to discuss and explore on own language development." He further notes,

"After acquiring knowledge in one's own language, it will be easier to understand the feelings of other languages... The importance of mother tongue will be clear in education from every point of view. Of course, it is a serious problem. Future of India depends on the possibility of vernacular language. For health, peace, freedom thought of Indian youth and for the performance of energy and vim, they should be given higher education in vernacular language and it cannot be ignored." (340, my trans)

These lines make it amply clear that he wanted to emphasize the importance of vernacular language that is Odia. In another journalistic writing or essay title is 'Not to Teach the Child in Vernacular Language is to Kill Them' he draws attention to exploitation of children by coercing them to study languages (other than their mother tongue) such as Hindi and English. Gopabandhu Das says that such imposition is as bad as killing the child. In this essay he appeals to people to solve this problem first by establishing Odia language as the medium of education especially at the level of primary education. By these journalistic writings he made wholehearted efforts to convey the importance of vernacular language, and that vernacular language provides easy access to knowledge. As a public intellectual he was doing a duty to make people conscious towards many national issues through his journalistic writings. Gopabandhu Das wrote many journalistic writings on Odia language and education. His encouraged writings such as 'New Monthly Magazine', 'Literature Society', 'Poverty and Students Life', 'Education and Agriculture' etc., reiterate his views on the indispensability of mother tongue.

Many intellectuals like Gopabandhu Das were working for social reform and the results were also visible. In Ganjam, Odia language was revived; in Sambalpur too, Odia language restored by the effort of Odia intelligentsia and Odia people in 1901. Effort for spread of education were successfully yielding results. Effort for social reform by newspapers and magazines gradually became one of the reasons of reformation in Odisha. Gopabandhu Das made efforts in many areas for social reformation. Pritish Acharya posits that the British government did not pay heed to any formal complaint, or application or petition but whenever people gathered for movements, the impact on the British government was conspicuous. Intellectuals like Gopabandhu understood it all too well. For this reason, he wrote many columns to provoke people to join in movements and some of these journal writings are 'Mukha Na Phitile Dukhajae Nanhi' (Nobody cares until You Speak Up), 'Jatiya Mahasratare Odia Mishu' (Let Odia be a Part of the National Mainstream), 'Sinha Bhumi Bhai Mananku Niras Kara Nanhi' (Don't disappoint Our Brothers from Sinha Bhumi) etc. He successfully managed to involve people both by his speech and his writings. In pre-independent times, less people were involved in different movements in Odisha. It was Gopabandhu the feisty columnist and impressive orator who transformed the movement into a largescale mass-movement.

To strengthen the agitation for a separate Odia province, he called for merging the movement with the nationalist struggle. He joined the Indian National Congress (INC) and took the leading responsibility in Odisha. In many of his journalistic writings he appealed to people to join the Congress, and because of his effort thousands of people started joining the Congress. The INC fought for national interest and had been successful in drawing the masses in its favour. That was also the reason why Gopabandhu Das got the large support from public. He wrote prolifically on the congress. Some of the writings include 'Utkala Samilani, join the Congress!', 'The Congress serves the Nation', 'Congress means everything to Odisha' etc. UUC (Utkal Samilani), which was one of the successful committees in Odisha for social reformation, was in danger (people started to suspect its morality and were withdrawing from it). The timely entry of Satyabadi which group gained the control over UUC saved the situation. Because of large public support, Satyabadi group gained control over it. Pritish Acharya writes that, "Gopabandhu's resolution was, however, passed with 127 votes in its favour and 16 against it. The UUC had been taken over by moderate nationalists. The UPCC was formed and the pledge for non-cooperation taken with great enthusiasm in Orissa." Some of his writings give a call for joining the UUC and some of his other writings focus on matters concerning the UUC.

Gopabandhu Das was a humanist rather than a nationalist and he was not in the favour of parochialism and he and some other intellectuals in this way never supported the opposition against Bengalis. Pritish Acharya contends,

Many of the young nationalist were probably vocal against parochialism because of their wide social exposure. Gopabandhu Das, Nilakantha Das, Godavarish Mishra, Krupasindhu Mishra and a few other had come in contact with many nationalist leaders of Bengal during the course of their education in Calcutta. (p-37)

The Gramscian notion of intellectual when applied on somebody like Gopabandhu, does not sound apt. According to Gramsci intellectuals are of two types, one is organic and another is traditional. Organic intellectuals are those who work for the class from which they belong to either in the present or in the past; and traditional intellectuals are those who are general and they are never confined to any particular class. On the one hand, Gopabandhu Das mostly dealt with the issues related to poor people and tried to offer help and ensure justice (especially through his journalistic writings) and he belonged to a poor family. In this way, we can call him organic intellectual. We also can call him organic intellectual in the context of Odisha because he mostly dealt with Odisha in both his speech and writings. On the other hand, he never confined himself to any class in society and he often dealt with national issues and in this way, he can be called a traditional intellectual. In many cases, we can find that different intellectuals from different area and from different economical background are involved in same type of work. According to situations, conditions(incidental) and surrounding problems (which are not according to economy condition) intellectuals take up matters.

As a public intellectual, Gopabandhu Das devoted his life to public. As we know, being a public intellectual is not a profession in itself and anybody who connected with people through intellectual engagement can be called a public intellectual. Gopabandhu Das completed his law degree then started his legal practice at Cuttack. But after a very short time he left the profession and started serving poor people of Odisha in the capacity of a social worker. He continued to visit many rural areas and helped the ones who were suffering. He totally connected with the people of rural areas. In this way we can call him a public intellectual. His experience of dealing directly with the public helped him to deal with public issues in his journalistic writings. He was writing journalistic writings not as a professional journalist but he was writing journalistic writings for social improvement and for this reason we cannot find any special literary language and special style in his journalistic writings. As a social worker he continued his social work through journalistic writings also. His social work and his journalistic writings are connected with each other. Before any social meeting or conference, he continued to give information on those programmes and also was appealing people to join in those programmes. He was getting more support for social service because of his journalistic writings. He succeeded in persuading people to involve in movements, and in many rich people to help financially for social work through his journalistic writings. He was not only dealing with the problems in his journalistic writings but also directly asking people to help in different social work. In some journalistic writings we can find that he was collecting donations from people for maintenance of different social institutions such as for Utkal Samilani and for Non-Cooperation movement and he even published the record of expenditure in his journalistic writings. Because of the trust the public reposed on him, he was successful in getting the financial support from people. He always admired people who were coming to the forefront for social work or for social improvement and also condemning those people directly for their lack of involvement. He encouraged different groups for work and for unity through his journalistic writings.

Gopabandhu's involvement in public affairs as journalist and a public intellectual draw our attention to important discourses of his times. At the level of the individual, what Gopabandhu did as a thinker and a social worker were remarkable. But more important is what we learn about certain discursive practices of the pre-independent times. If there was one thing which was common to some of the major figures of the nationalist struggle, it was that they were journalists. Nehru, Gandhi and even Ambedkar (whose journalistic oeuvre has received scant attention from scholars) wrote columns and were editors too. The other ubiquitous profession was law. Gandhi, Nehru, Patel, Ambedkar and Gopabandhu were all lawyers. The choice of profession could be anything but incidental. Both law and journalism were instruments of modernity and both were considered effective tools to deal with British injustice. But the domain of the letters remained restricted to a select few and perhaps needed more time to make their presence felt on a wider scale. Between the rabidity of the extremists and the doggedly constitutional methods of the moderates, Gandhi had chosen a path which demanded steady perseverance and was radical in questioning the legitimacy of the institutions which colonial modernity had introduced to India. Gandhi's practice of combining prolific writing with active social work lent itself amenable to an emerging public sphere which was located in the interstices of tradition and modernity. Besides, using the print medium for spreading a social message was also Gandhi's way of rescuing journalism from dour professionalism. Gopabandhu Das provincialized what was an integral part of the Gandhian national struggle.

CHAPTER THREE

Journalist as Public Intellectual in Post-Independent Time; In the Case of Surendra Mohanty

Surendra Mohanty (1922-1990) belongs to different time and different society from those of Gopabandhu Das'. Gopabandhu Das died in 1928 while Surendra Mohanty was born in 1922. Surendra Mohanty born in June 21, 1922 at Puruso Mopura village in Cuttack district. He belonged to an educated family and some of the men in the previous generation had been good Sanskrit scholars. He spent his childhood in rural environment. He was not interested in study during his childhood but gradually he became a good student. During his school time he joined a Non-Cooperation conference despite tight restrictions and again he slunk from hostel to meet Jawaharlal Nehru. He got the death news of Madhusudan Das in 1934 and he got hurt by that news very much and his love for Madhu Babu did not end in his entire life. He wrote two volume biographies of Madhusudan Das; one is *Satabdira Surya* (Light of the Century)and another is *Kulabrudha* (The Old Patriarch). He participated in political rallies during his school time. He was quite impulsive even as a child and often broke rules and regulations.

After his school he took admission in Ravenshaw College and lived in a mess. He also started his writer career from that time. In his mess he made two best friends: Binod Chandra Nayak and Guruprasad Mohanty who also took interest in literature and later became renowned poets themselves. During his third year of college his story 'Men and Economics' got published in *Arati* journal; this was his first published story. He continued his literary pursuit relentlessly. He got 100 silver coins as prize from 'Maharaja Janmastoba Committee', which had been instituted in the memory of the king of Baripada, for his drama *Pruthi Balabha*. He left his college education to participate in Quit-India movement. He started his career as a visiting agent of a silk company but he left his job and then started offering tuition classes to earn a living. He started his journalistic career in a journal called *New Odisha,* in which he reviewed the drama *Atibadi Jagannath Das* and for his endeavor, he received positive response from readers. Then he worked as a proof reader for *New Odisha*. While working as a proof reader, he got exposed to a wide range of journalistic writings which expanded his knowledge in this field. But indeed, he started his real journalist career in *The Observer* which had been started by Madhusudan Mohanty and was the only English journal at that time. He quickly rose to fame as a journalist and as a writer in Odisha. Until much later in his career, he had little professional stability and therefore he had to switch from one newspaper to another. Even when he had settled in a successful career, he had to manage three jobs- writing, journalism and politics. Mohanty was a member of Parliament. He spent most of his time as a journalist. He was jailed for his satirical journalistic writings against government and against corruption. In a journal title *Janata,* he wrote satirical stories against government under the heading 'Balingara Nero' (The Nero of Balinga) where Balinga clearly refers to Kalinga (the name used for ancient Odisha and some of the adjoining areas). The Nero in the story was chief minister Harekrushna Mahatab and the other character Gabakrushna referred to the famous socialist and political leader Nabakrushna Choudhury. The character Lengada Birabhradra was a fictional version of Biren Mitra. He stayed in jail for 39 days and after his release he again started the *Janata* (Janata was owned by Madhusudan Mohanty but was controlled and managed by Surendra Mohanty). After jail he started that journal with his own effort and money. He had to struggle hard to revive the journal. He admits in his autobiography that most of what he wrote in Janata was based mostly on his real-life experience. He wrote most of his journalistic writings as stories and rest as articles.

Surendra Mohanty was mainly a writer and politics entered his life later and kept him preoccupied for a fairly long time. Direct and active involvement in politics meant traveling to various parts of Odisha and meeting people regularly. Politics enriched his experience and helped him understand the society and its administration better. As I discussed above that he used to join in political rallies from his childhood. Despite a busy political schedule, he devoted time to writing. Surendra Mohanty also deal with the problems and issues of people at that time. Even though both Surendra Mohanty and Gopabandhu were, technically speaking journalists and politicians, their respective milieu was different and so was their approach to their profession.

Surendra Mohanty started his journalistic career during 1945 in the English Journal *New Odisha* in which he wrote a review on the drama *Atibadi Jagannath Das*. But full-fledged journalism, for him, started in 1945 with the journal *The Observer* and achieved the fame of writer and journalist in Odisha. We can see that he started his journalist career just two years before India eventually became independent in 1947 and he spent most of his journalist career in post-independent time. So, before assessing his career and reputation as a journalist and public intellectual, we have to know the social, political and cultural landscape of Odisha (and India) in the post-independent period.

After years of struggle, India finally attained freedom from British rule in 1947. But freedom did not automatically imply complete eradication of every problem facing the society. If not anything else, the fact that independence was accompanied by communal violence and bloodshed, left a lot that the newly formed nation had to grapple with. Besides, major problems such as starvation of poor people, poverty, crisis in education, corruption etc. had to be dealt with. But we also can find a lot of changes in post-independent India. In this chapter we need to understand Surendra Mohanty's journalist career, especially that phase of career when journalism itself had undergone significant changes in the period following independence.

The tradition of printing newspapers had started close to two centuries before India became independent. In 1780, James Augustus started the English newspaper The *Bengal Gadget* from West Bengal. From that time newspapers had been established in various parts of India.

Newspaper played a big role in the freedom movement and in initiating social reformation. During late nineteenth century newspapers prevailed in a large number in different part of India. In Odisha also, many newspapers started during 19th century. A printing press had been set up in Cuttack under the aegis of the missionaries in 1838 and the first published tract was meant to provide information on pilgrimage to Puri during Jagannath's car festival. But more emphatically, it dissuaded people from undertaking an arduous journey and instead prodded them to choose Christ as their God. But as mentioned before hand-written newspaper existed as early as 1769 in Odisha. *Kujibar Patrika* written by Sadhu Sundar Das had been quite a sensation in its times and had later been translated by none other than Amos Sutton, the man who had played an instrumental role in introducing print in Odisha. In the aftermath of the famine, the first printed newspaper *Utkal Dipika* came into being. It was run by Gauri Shankar Ray. Within a span of roughly ninety years, a lot had changed in journalism and in production and circulation of newspapers. In post-independent Odisha, newspapers got more important roles in society. In post-independent era, more than seven newspapers were dealing with public issues by which both people and government were affected. Newspapers were very close to people by giving information to people and by giving various knowledge. Because of election system or vote power of people, newspapers got more importance in post-independent time. Newspapers were creating consciousness in people and indirectly influenced election results. Cynics saw this as a corrupting influence. What is worth noting is that the major newspapers in Odisha post 1947 have been owned by political heavyweights. Partisanship is a common cavil against them. While the allegations cannot be dismissed easily, one also cannot ignore the contribution of newspapers towards reformations and in drawing attention towards serious problems. The grouse that comes from the other side of the editorial desk is increasing censorship of media. Even after independence, newspapers could not enjoy full freedom. Very often the press came in the line of fire for having openly critiqued the state. In 1951 'The Press Act' introduced by government was perceived as a serious blow to freedom of newspapers. Again in 1975, Indira Gandhi imposed Emergency in India when newspapers could not get any freedom and many journalists suffered for their anti-government writings. Surendra Mohanty was also jailed for his satirical writings against corruption in which the government of that time seemed to have been complicit. We can find that many newspapers support and admire government instead of speaking the truth and, in this way, gradually the credibility of press came under question. Newspapers became commercialized after independence. Because of increase in readership, many newspapers made good profit. Journalism became a coveted profession. During the time of Gopabandhu Das, intellectuals, nationalists and social reformers were journalists. It would be hard to find someone whose sole profession was journalism and who was renowned for being a journalist. The professionalization of journalism also accorded unprecedented fame to journalists. When reformers wrote for newspapers, their columns had charted their paths to fame but with increasing commercialization of newspapers and professionalization of journalism, public figures and intellectuals were often requested to contribute to newspapers. The opinions were considered important in terms of who was making them.

It would be important here to pay attention to the emergence of new political parties in India and what bearing it had on the fate of journalism in India. For the expansion of the political field in order to accommodate more players also diversified opinions. The new parties that came up also needed their mouthpieces. So, competitiveness in journalism also went hand in hand with struggle for political power. After the full independent, Harekrushna Mahatab became the first chief minister of Odisha after India gained independence. Locally and nationally many parties were coming into existence. Revolts, movements, pickets continued even after independence. One of the major movements happened in 1966 historically called Padmapur, Kalahandi movement organized by socialists (this drew attention to famine problems) against government of Odisha. After freedom another important organization which influenced people was Rastriya Swayam Sevak Sangh (R.S.S.) which had been accused of being involved in the assassination of Mahatma Gandhi. In 1980, another big national political party emerged; it was the Bharatiya Janata Party (BJP). The political parties that came into existence after independence ascended to power in various parts of India. In 1964, a largescale students' movement gathered momentum as it protested vociferously against the corruption of the Congress Government. In 1975 Indira Gandhi declared Emergency without any strong reason. Political leaders from the opposition were sent to jail. Newspapers and press did not get any freedom during this time. In 1977 Emergency ended. During and after the period of emergency the history of journalism had taken a decisive turn, for never before had the state been so repressive in its efforts to muzzle voices of dissent. On the other hand, there were media houses that showed slavish loyalty to the government and toed its line obediently. Journalists stood divided and competitive rivalry was also met with ideological differences.

If independence marked the dawn of a new era for journalism, literary aesthetics too evolved in new ways. Publication of literary works increased. Literary works found new platforms. Writings were getting published not only in books but also in many journals and newspapers. Poetries were getting published in a large number both in press and books. One well known Odia poet Sachidananda Routray in his essay title 'For Modern and Post-Modern' wrote that

On the one hand, dishonest and imbecile men are misusing freedom and abusing power in the field of politics, on the other hand, some silly men have become poets overnight by writing bad poetry on freedom. So even though the way for modern poems is clear, it is not free of danger. (Routray 91)

Some of the famous Odia poets of this age are Sachidananda Routray, Jagannath Prasad Das, Benudhar Rout, Dipak Mishra, Sarat Chandra Pradhan, Pratibha Satpathi etc., all who set new trends in poetry.

Story writing also took a turn in the positive direction around this time. During this time, we can find reality in many stories which are based on contemporary societies and conditions. Here Surendra Mohanty' name comes first who gives the story writing a new mode. In his stories, we can find the problems and emotions of men being expressed in elegant and moving prose. He wrote many satirical stories which focusing on democratic principles of Odisha and India. The stories were often realistic. He gave new direction to story writing during post-independent period. His famous contemporaries include Rajkishore Ray, Kishori Charan Das, Manoj Das, Nilamani Sahu, Akhila Mohan Patnayak, Achyutananda Satpathi, Kailash Patnaik et al. Among them Manoj Das and Kishori Charan Das went on to become internationally acclaimed writers. Manoj Dash known for his presentation of feelings, subject and style in his stories. Kishore Charan is well known for his presentation of the middle-class. He clearly gives the picture of post-independent Odisha such as the miseries of men, life-experience, situation, mental condition etc.

In the field of novel, we cannot see any progress like poetry and story writing in post-independent time. But some novelist wrote novels which gained good reputation within and outside the country. Two such famous novelists are Gopinath Mohanty and Surendra Mohanty. The essay also fared well. Establishment of many newspapers and journals aided the progress of the essay form. Essay was popular in newspapers and journals. Harekrushna Mahatab wrote essays in *Prajatantra* magazine under the heading 'Village Pleasure'. Then other Odia newspapers such as *Pragatibadi, Dharitri, Sambad* etc. made essay more popular. Surendra Mohanty wrote essays under the heading 'Sesastambha' (The Last Column) in *Sambad*. He wrote other essays under other headings such as "Narottama Chakada" and "Anya Drustire". He wrote almost all essays in newspapers and journals. Later in this chapter I will discuss on his essays broadly. Other writers such as Manoj Das wrote his columns under the heading 'Kete Diganta' (The Endless Horizon), Nilamani Sahu wrote under the heading 'Devdasara Drustipata' (Devadasa's Gaze).

The field of Criticism progressed due to establishment of different educational institutions. Establishment of Utkal

University in 1943, publication of *Jhankar* journal in 1949, establishment of Odisha Literature Academy in 1958, starting of Sambalpur University and Berhampur University in 1967 and many others which created an environment conducive to critical thinking. Some critics who made effort in this field are Krushna Chandra Panigrahi, Kunjabihari Tripathy, Bansidhara Mohanty, Kanhu Charan Mishra, Gangadhara Bal et al. Drama also progressed well. Some well-known dramatists are Pranabandhu Kar, Biswajit Das, Bijaya Mishra, Banabihari Panda, Kartik Chandra Ratha et al.

Effort towards development of education was started well before independence. Intellectuals like Fakir Mohan Senapati, Gopabandhu Das and many other started establish education from pre-independent time which I have discussed in third chapter of this dissertation. From that time, it had been continued after independence also. But after freedom, schools were established by government and got financial support which helped for educational development. To involve every child into education, government started enrolment drive during 1960-62. Many schools, colleges and universities were established by government to develop education in Odisha. But we can also find many defects in education system. According to survey in 1995, from every 100 students 46 students left education before class-v. In the field of education also we can see corruption. But education facilities were rapidly growing after independent.

Economic situation of Odisha was too bad after independence also. Odisha was the poorest state of India in after-independent time. In this way we can see the journalistic time of Surendra Mohanty i.e., post-independent time. Surendra Mohanty mostly dealt with above discussed issues in his journalistic writings. We can know a journalist public intellectual more clearly by getting the knowledge of his/her society and time.

Surendra Mohanty wrote many journalistic writings. He wrote his satirical pieces under the heading 'Balingara Niro' against the corruption of government. At that time Dr Harekrushna Mahatab was chief minister of Odisha, whom Surendra Mohanty satirized under the name 'Niro' and for his satire he was sent to jail. Again, he was writing satire later in *The Sambad* newspaper under the heading 'Narottama Chakada'. He wrote many journalistic writings under the heading 'Sesastambha' and under the heading 'Anyadrustire'.

Under the heading of 'Narottama Chakada', we can discuss the article of 11 November 1984. In this story we can see that a king living in a Mutt (a Hindu religious institution) and his servant Madhia who spies for king and gives the various information of his area. Here we can find picture of a society and people. Inside this story we can see that a 14-year girl is killed and within short time without investigation some people burn that dead body. Then king gets this information from Madhia and king started making sound by cymbal after hear this information. By the cymbal sound, people gather near king and then king describes the danger and criminals name by singing a song. Throughout this story we can find a satirical picture of that time. As I discussed above that in post-independent time corruption and criminal were on the rise and this story seems to satirize the society of that time. This story satirizes the role of the king and people who are silent and afraid of speaking against criminals. In next Sunday story of 'Narottama Chakada', we can see the same character, same area picture but it presents other issues of that society. Here we can see that the king getting information on corruption and criminals but is not taking any action and he is busy in making sound by cymbals and also busy in talking and gossiping. Here we can say that the writer gives the picture of the society of his time that kings are unable to stop the crime and corruption of some powerful people. Inside story we also can see that people are only talking but no one opposing crime or corruption openly and we can say that this is also a satire on people of that time. On 25 November 1984, the story is continued and we see that the king only plays cymbals and is busy chatting like previous story. His devotee Dama is beaten by watchman of a zamindar but the king says that he would make the condition of opposition very bad by playing cymbals and in the last part he keeps singing and playing cymbal. We can see the satire on the leaders or kings who while away their time abdicating their responsibilities and are too scared to face criminals of the society. Writer satirizes his society and time by telling stories and by fictional characters. Playing cymbals and chanting mantras are Hindu rituals and we know that these rituals are seen in most villages of India especially in Odisha and we can notice that this story satirizes those people who only perform religious rituals and do nothing to improve the society. We also take this story as the satire on political leaders who are unable to stop criminals and other corruption and remain indifferent towards these problems. Surendra Mohanty presented the real pictures of the society of his time through these stories. He also satirizes the Mutt system through these stories.

His other column is 'Sesastambha' under the heading of which he wrote more than the two hundred journalistic pieces in *The Sambad*. Under this heading he wrote mostly on literature and other writings on social issues. First, I would like to discuss his writings on literature. He was so concerned about his mother tongue that is Odia language. His first article under 'Sesastambha' heading is 'We and the Odia Language'. Here he says that Odia language should be developed according to time. Language is not meant to be static and it gets enriched with time as it interacts with other languages. For example, in the Odia that is in use today, we do not find many words and usages which were prevalent in the time of Markanda Das and Sarala Das. Many words came to Odia language from Mughal, Maratha and English during their reign in Odisha. (Mohanty, my trans, 17) He opposes those who do not support use of some English word in Odia language for better understanding. Some English words which Odia people will understand better than Odia language such as 'executive engineer', 'secretariat', 'writ' etc. He mourns for the reason that there is no standard dictionary on Odia language without which language development is not possible. He states in the last part of this article that different universities in Odisha, literary bodies and other institutions should take interest in publishing a standard Odia Dictionary because the development of language depends on them. (Mohanty, my trans, 17-19). Public intellectuals show their interest in different fields of society and Surendra Mohanty shows his interest more in the standardization of Odia language and Odia literature. In 'Wretched Litterateur' he raised the important issue in literature. Here he talks on the wretched or suffering writers. He says that the writers cannot adjust themselves with the economic competition in society. But their struggle and agony inspire people and raise their consciousness. He also says that even after government's helping policy, many wretched writers are not finding help from government because of corruption. So, he appeals to establish an autonomous selection board like 'England Royal Literary Fund' which would be constructed only by writers and they will select and provide fund to writers who need. As a writer, Surendra Mohanty also suffered from many problems in his life. In next article title 'The Garland of Literature' he discusses the real value of award for a writer. He does not disparage awards but contends that the responses and love of readers is the real award. In next article title 'Literature and Society' he says that in every era writers or litterateurs take the responsibility to change society. He says that society never change by votes or politicians' speech. This is the responsibility of a writer. In this article he encourages writers to play active role in bringing changes in the society. He also appeals to the writers to make realism a part of their creative exercise rather than postmodernism, since the former can potentially help to change society. Here we can see that Surendra Mohanty gives importance to both the development of literature and society. In his other article 'Messenger of Soul' he discusses the importance of translation in enriching literature of a language. There are many scholars in India and also in Odisha whose great literary works are unknown to world because their works are not translated to other languages especially to English language. He says that in European literature especially in American literature we can find a vast number of translations of great works of different areas of the world. He mourns for the fact that in Odisha the field of translation is very poor and it is rare to come across great works of translation. A translation can make an original work better and more interesting. Hallador Laxness, novelist and translator of Iceland, got the Nobel prize for his translation. He finally quotes the lines of Alexander Pushkin's that translation is "The couriers of human spirit". In this article we can see that Surendra Mohanty emphasizes the field of translation in literature and appeals to the writers to follow this field also. He wrote many articles and every article shows new aspect or issue of literature and in most of them he gives messages and ideas to develop different field of literature. After some years of independence, the novel had acquired a respectable position in the Odia literary field because during that time novelist like Kalindi Charan Panigrahi, Kanhucharan Mohanty and Gopinath Mohanty were producing great novels but during 1980s this field practically lay vacant. To address this issue, Surendra Mohanty wrote the article 'The Novel-Problem'. He says that in contemporary novels, there are more sex issues and cheap love. Such type of novel may give pleasure to the readers but serious readers and critics will not like these. He says that contemporary novelists have no deep feelings and emotions except for those which are superficial. There is lack of knowledge on life and incidents in contemporary novelists. In 'Victory Voyage of Youth' article he deals with a universal issue. Here he appeals to the youth to do something great. He says that Mahatma Gandhi had made agreement with General Scott in South Africa and got the leader post before 30 years. In England-History, Edward the Black Prince won 'the Battle of Crecy' award when he was 16-year-old. Evan the Terrible got the post of king when he was 17-year-old. Alexander got 'the great' fame before 21 years. (Mohanty, my trans, 56) He again says that this voyage of youth is also seen in literature field; Shakespeare (1564) as a great dramatist proved himself before 27. Milton (1658) wrote great work like *Lycidas* before 30. French dramatist Moliere

(1627) successfully rivalled Shakespeare as a dramatist even before he was twenty-three years of age. Jane Austen (1775) died at the age of forty-seven but before that she had already achieved the fame of great novelist. Goethe (1749) wrote *Faust* at the age of twenty-four. Wordsworth (1770) wrote almost all famous poems before the age of 48. (Mohanty, my trans, 57) Here he describes the value of the youth time and describes it with many examples to show that what he is saying is not unreal and that youth should be spent on great things.

In some of the articles of '*Seshastambha*' (The Last Column) we can find the picture of contemporary society. In an article entitled 'Other India' he mentions that he always held the belief that love was a matter of heart and could be felt only by heart. But after watching programs on Doordarshan (Government of India's. television channel) he discovered to his amazement that love entails dancing, singing, showing thighs and waist, and singing in a melodious voice. In the same article, he reports that his domestic help started weeping when s/he saw children on television enjoying their meals but her grandsons and granddaughters were starving at home. In his 'Discover India' article he describes the good and the bad of India. The article was written on the occasion of Pope's visit to India. He says that he has thousands of allegations against television but he thanks the television for broadcasting the Pope's visit to India. He says that Pope becomes emotional after reach to India. Writer says that there is no acting in that emotion of Pope. India was holy place of many great monks like Gautama Buddha and many great men like Mahatma Gandhi. Christ himself is said to have spent twelve years of his life in India. Once India had enlightened Europe with its knowledge and culture. But today India is left with video, colorful television, disco dance, obscenity, economic disparity, violence and terrorism. On the other hand, intellectuals from the West come to India to learn about the land of Buddha, Shankaracharya and Gandhi. (Mohanty, my trans, 143-144)

His other column is 'Anyadrustire' (The Other Point of View) and under this heading he wrote many articles which were based on his contemporary society and politics. On 7th August 1987, he wrote 'I Just Want a Single-Room House' where he wrote on the situations of honest prime-minister especially on the situation of Gulzarilal Nanda who had no home to stay even after having served as a two-time Prime-Minister. Now he is searching for a home to stay in his very old age. He then mentions Jawaharlal Nehru who lived by the royalty he received and Lal Bahadur Shastri who suffered more than Gulzarilal Nanda because of his honesty. On the other hand, Surendra Mohanty says that they are not fatuous but so honest for which they all suffered. He says that such type of people can save democracy. But affluent politicians cannot do anything for the country. In the next article 'President and Constitution' he clearly writes that Indian presidents' have no power and take the vow to save constitution just for namesake. He says that Dr Fakhruddin Ali Ahmed unhesitatingly signed the file which allowed the imposition of Emergency by Indira Gandhi. He says that president are namely and decoratively president and no president ever used power to save constitution. In next article he discusses the corruption in Jagannath temple in Puri, Odisha. In his article 'Fake Certificate and Job' he describes the problems that many people get job by fake certificate. Here we can see that writer discusses the corruption in the field of education. In this way he deals with many contemporary social issues and political issues under the heading 'Anyadrustire' published in *The Sambada*.

We can analyze Surendra Mohanty as public intellectual by taking his journalistic writings. He spent time in politics also and had attended many public campaigns and gave many speeches but those public relations were purely for political motive. In real sense he connected with people by his writings especially by his journalistic writings. We can put the definition of public intellectual of Romila Thapar in the case of Surendra Mohanty. Thapar says that, "Public intellectuals frequently concern themselves with issues related to human rights and to the functioning of society, such that it ensures the primacy of social justice." (Thapar 61) As a journalist Surendra Mohanty deals with public issues and many social issues in both his journal articles and stories. He focuses on and blames the exploitations of poor people by corruption. He wrote many journalistic writings on corruption. He knew political corruptions very well and his political background helped him to deal with those issues vividly. We can say that there is social justice in the journalistic writings of Surendra Mohanty. He did not do any partiality to any class and deals the major problems of his time. One important thing we can discuss in the case of public-intellectuals that they always follow rational process of thought and often give possible solutions to many problems. Surendra Mohanty totally follows the rational process of thought and we cannot find any blind belief which he follows in his writings. We can find many writings in which he proposes solutions to many problems. A public intellectual always raises his voice against social problems and peoples' problems. As a public intellectual he raises voice against many social problems in his journalistic writings and often writes to improve those situations which I have discussed above. If we take the view of Antonio Gramsci, Surendra Mohanty may not fit exactly into the categories defined by Gramsci. He can be called an organic intellectual because he mostly deals with the problems of Odisha and Odia people. But on the other hand, we cannot find any special class which he presents in his journalistic writings and deals with any problems which he feels important to deal and, in this way, we can call him a traditional intellectual. Antonio says that organic intellectuals deal with the problems of a class in a society and those intellectuals belongs to that class in present time or in past time. Surendra Mohanty did not deal with any special class and in this way, he would come under the category of traditional intellectual. Another important point to discuss a public intellectual is the character. In the book The Public Intellectual in India, it is written that, "A teacher can still do an excellent job of teaching something without necessarily doing that thing well- for example, a coach need not be a great player but can mould great players. But a public intellectual is not in that position and she has to embody the virtues she desires of others." (184) A public intellectual should follow the moralities or any other things he writes or speaks for people to follow. As a public intellectual Surendra Mohanty was far away from corruption and opposed corruption in his journalistic writings. He wrote many journalistic articles to develop literature in Odisha and was respected as a writer of the first order.

Surendra Mohanty's journey as a journalist and a public intellectual also maps the turns and changes in the two respective fields following India's attainment of independence in 1947. Whereas in the case of somebody like Gopabandhu Das we had seen a reformer using the print medium to spread his message and to bolster his activism using a modern tool, in the case of Mohanty it is essentially a man of letter who takes up the responsibility of raising social awareness. Between the two lie the transformation of a profession, a newly formed nation which expresses itself through the print medium, and the rise of what would continue to present itself as the representative the nation's collective aspiration- the educated middle class.

CHAPTER FOUR

An Assessment

This dissertation has elaborately discussed the changing notions of public intellectuals in idea with the broad argument that the changes were factored by the emergence of a new nation, the rise of a new middle class which largely came to be identified as the public, whose aspirations were presumed to be the collective aspiration of the public, and the reformer/activist gave writer way to the category of 'men of letters' who were commentators first and not necessarily social workers or activists. I also argue that public intellectuals directly or indirectly depend on the social structure of their time and those social structures shape the works of intellectuals and public intellectuals.

To understand the notion 'public intellectual', this study discussed other related important concepts clearly in the first chapter. Public, public sphere and public intellectual are connected with each other. There is no proper historical evidence of the starting of these concepts. Habermas provides historical reasons for the evolution of public sphere in Europe. We cannot claim that public sphere tradition started in the modern world because of advancement of many things. But in modern world, diverse and disparate social structures, technologies, political discourses boost the public sphere. We can find in the history that under the reign of some kings or queens there are freedom and respect for public discussions and public sphere. Queen Elizabeth I in England gave freedom to the people for discussion and other things by which at that time literature could scale new heights. Similarly, the tradition of public intellectual is not new. In ancient Greece, Socrates was the finest example of a public intellectual who continued to share his thought with people by visiting many areas and many people to improve the social situations.

There are no social living system or society system in ancient time and without that system the notion 'public', 'public sphere' and 'public intellectual' are not possible. Without the connection (means people come into contact with each other and connected with each other for some reason) system of people we cannot find the notion 'public' possible. After 'society' and 'public' systems, other systems such as 'state', 'politics', 'public groups and institutions', 'public discussion', 'public sphere', 'public intellectual' etc. become possible. So, these are all deeply related to society and people. I take particularly three concepts to discuss in this chapter such as 'public', 'public sphere' and 'public intellectual'. To understand the main concept of this dissertation that is 'public intellectual' we need to understand the other two mentioned concepts. For this reason, I take these concepts to discuss in my first chapter.

Public intellectual and public sphere are related to each other and help each other to succeed in their field. Public sphere is the discussion of a group of people on some important social issues and try to find solutions to problems. Using the public sphere, the active participants became public intellectuals. After the establishment of newspapers and journals, number of public discussions increased and many intellectual started to communicate their thought with people through these media. Public intellectuals play a great role to raise awareness among people on different issues through the medium of newspapers and journals. Gopabandhu Das, whom I have defined as journalist public intellectual, used the medium of newspaper to involve people in different activities surrounding the creation of a separate Odia province and the nationalist movement at large, such as in Utkal Samilani, in Congress Meetings, and in various social meetings. Thoughts of many intellectuals make people realize on different issues and create spheres and discussions among people. People also get those thought seriously and proceed to discuss on those which are important need for them. In this way, public intellectuals also care on the important issues of people and their society.

As I have discussed in aforementioned chapter that there is a difference we can find between public intellectual and the journalist as a public intellectual. Public intellectuals are intellectuals who communicate their thought with people by attending public conferences, meetings and by visiting people directly, by writing books. But journalist public intellectuals are intellectuals who communicate their thought with people by the medium of newspapers and journals. One journalist public intellectual may use other media too. One public intellectual who communicates with people by his books or other writings, we can view him as the-writer-as-a-public-intellectual. Surendra Mohanty, whose life and works have been discussed in this project, was also a writer-public-intellectual who wrote many stories and essays based on public and social issues. His novel *Andha Diganta* is based on the post-independent time of Odisha which mostly reflects on corruption in Odisha.

In my second chapter entitled 'Journalist as Public Intellectual in Pre-Independent Times: The Case of Gopabandhu Das', I take Gopabandhu Das to discuss as a journalist public intellectual. Here we can find that as an intellectual, his different actions and works are the products of his time. Like many others, he was also concerned with the situations of his time and tried to solve many situations of his time that is the pre-independent time in India and Odisha. Every public intellectual deal with the issues which are directly or indirectly related with people. Intellectuals can deal with the issues of any time (past, present and future) but every public intellectual deal with the issues related with the people of contemporary time. A public intellectual mostly shaped by his/her society structure and time. Gopabandhu Das was also shaped by his contemporary society and time. As a journalist public intellectual, he was using the medium of newspapers and journal for the improvement of the situations of his time. He was a devoted social worker. He used the medium of newspaper to continue that social service and to cover a large number of people. Journalist public intellectuals access a large number of people within a short period of time. Newspaper is the most effective medium which has a big role to change many things in a society. Gopabandhu Das used the medium of the newspaper effectively.

The third chapter deals with the Surendra Mohanty as a journalist public intellectual and also deals with his time that is after independence. In this chapter I have thrown light on changing social structure after independence, in order to understand Surendra Mohanty as a journalist public intellectual. It is important to know the social structure and time of a public intellectual to understand him. Surendra Mohanty was mainly a writer and secondly, he was an editor, a journalist and a politician. Like Gopabandhu Das he also dealt with the major issues of his time. As a litterateur, he mostly writes journalistic writings on literature issues to improve the conditions and situations of his time. Here we can understand one common point that both Gopabandhu Das and Surendra Mohanty influenced by their professional knowledge and work and write many journalistic articles related to their professional field. Both follow simple process and tricks for improvement of many situations in their journalistic writings.

Works of different public intellectuals differ from each other because of various factors. We can find many reasons that why journalistic writings of Gopabandhu Das are different from Surendra Mohanty. One major fact is the social structure. Time of Das is the pre-independent time and Mohanty's time is post-independent time (I take his journalistic career time which is the post-independent period) and their situations, problems, conditions and structure of society were different. Another reason is profession and these both intellectuals belong to different professions. Gopabandhu Das was a trained lawyer and social worker by choice whereas Surendra Mohanty is especially a writer and we can find the influence of these intellectuals in their journalistic writings. Except all these, everybody has different life experience which also a reason for different views and works of different public intellectuals. But common thing is that every public intellectual tries to improve or solve the problems and situations in the field which they deal with. Readers of this book can get clear ideas on how to continue public intellectualism with different difficult situations. Especially, the way they made their lives as well as their service as public intellectual activity sustainable in threatening situation is a phenomenal road map to the future public intellectuals.

Notes

1 Enlightenment: The Enlightenment was a movement of 18ᵗʰ century Europe when a revolution in knowledge and fact happened.

2 Bengal Gazette: Bengal Gazette was the first newspaper of India published from West-Bengal. Gazette means the letter of kings or queens.

3 Utkala Mani: Jewel of Odisha. Gopabandhu Das is called Utkala Mani in Odisha.

4 Social Structure: Various things by which a society is running or constructed.

5 Panchasakha: five friends. Gopabandhu Das, Harihara Das, Nilakantha Das, Krupasindhu Mishra, Godabarish Mishra are known as Pancha Sakha and their time is known as Pancha Sakha period in literature and in history of Odisha.

6 Padma Shree Award: It is the fourth highest civilian award in the Republic of India given by the Government of India in Republic Day every year.

7 Platonic Concept: Concepts of Plato. Plato was a philosopher in ancient Greece. He is famous for his various philosophy in the World.

8 Dictatorship: A type of Government where one individual or a group od individual get the ruling power in a country.

9 Secular Notion: Idea of secular system. Secular means where all religions are taken as same. Habermas primarily thought that non-secular discussions cannot be called public sphere but later he cancelled this idea and he felt that religious discussions also help to solve many problems in a society.

10 Na-Anka Famine: It was the danger famine of 1866 in Odisha which famine took more than one million lives.

11 Paika Rebellion: Paika is a caste in Odisha known for their brave nature. By the leadership of Bakshi Jagabandhu in 1817, a rebellion movement started against the British rule in Odisha. In that rebellion most of the Paikas were participated and for that reason it is called Paika Rebellion.

12 Gadjat: Tributary or feudatory states of Odisha during British rule is known as Gadjat state or area.

13 Academic Intellectuals: Intellectuals who do jobs in academics such as in Universities, educational Institutions, other institutions.

14 Zamindars: Land lords or seigniory in Odisha are called zamindars.

15 Gurukula System of Education: Gurukula educations system is a Indian ancient educational system where education provides under tree or in nunneries where students were learnt to obey teachers and to do devotion for teacher. Here students do their own work. Here mythology discussions are regularly happening.

16 Satyabadi Group: Satyabadi is an area of Odisha from where Gopabandhu Das along with some friends started a school named Satyabadi School. Gopabandhu and his other companion used to do extracurricular work from that school such as relief distribution, newspaper publish, various social meetings etc. Gopabandhu Das and this group known as Satyabadi Group.

17 Gramscian Notion: Ideas of Antonio Gramsci. Antonio Gramsci was a Italian Marxist philosopher and a politician. I used his notion of public intellectual in this dissertation.

18 Janata: People

19 Utkal: Old name of the state Odisha

Sources

Acharya, Pritish. *National Movement and Politics in Orissa, 1920-29*. Mathura Road, New Delhi, India: SAGE Publications, 2008. (E-book)

Das, Gopabandhu. *Gopabandhu Chayanika*, ed. Pritish Acharya. Vasantkunj, New Delhi: National Book Trust, India, 2009.

Das, Gourahari. *Sahitya O Sambadikatara Swarnasetu: Surendra Mohanty* (unpublished dissertation). Bhubaneswar, Odisha.

Edgar, Andrew. *Habermas; The Key Concepts*. Park Square, Milton Park, Abingdon, Oxon: Routledge, 2006. (E-book)

Habermas, Jurgen. *The Structural Transformation of the Public Sphere*, trans., Thomas Burger. Cambridge, Massachusetts: The MIT Press, 1991. (E-book)

Mohanty, Surendra. *Patha O Pruthibi*. Binodbehari, Cuttack: Friends' Publisher, 2017.

Mohanty, Surendra. *Sesastambha*. Bapuji Nagar, Bhubaneswar: Ama Odisha, 2017.

Mohanty, Surendra. "Anya Drustire." *The Sambada*, Bhubaneswar, 7 August 1987, pp 4.

Mohanty, Surendra. "Anya Drustire." *The Sambada*, Bhubaneswar, 14 August 1987, pp 4.

Mohanty, Surendra. "Anya Drustire." *The Sambada*, Bhubaneswar, 21 August 1987, pp 4.

Mohanty, Surendra. "Anya Drustire." *The Sambada*, Bhubaneswar, 28 August 1987, pp 4.

Mohanty, Surendra. "Anya Drustire." *The Sambada*, Bhubaneswar, 11 September 1987, pp 4.

Mohanty, Surendra. "Anya Drustire." *The Sambada*, Bhubaneswar, 25 September 1987, pp 4.

Mohanty, Surendra. "Narottama Chakada." *The Sambada*, Bhubaneswar, 11 November 1984.

Mohanty, Surendra. "Narattama Chakada." *The Sambada*, Bhubaneswar, 18 November 1984.

Mohanty, Surendra. "Narattama Chakada." *The Sambada*, Bhubaneswar, 25 November 1984.

Mohanty, Surendra. "Narattama Chakada." *The Sambada*, Bhubaneswar, 2 December 1984.

Panigrahi, Shiva. *Swadhinata Para Odisha*. Maitri Sarani, Cuttack: The Institute of Oriental and Orissan Studies, 1997.

Small, Hellen. *The Public Intellectual*. Cawley Road, Oxford, UK: Blackwell Publishers, 2002. (E-book)

Thapar, Ramila. *The Public Intellectual in India*. Dhruv Raina, Peter Ronald Desouza, Neeladri Bhattacharya, Jawed Naqvi. Daryaganj, New Delhi: Aleph Book Company, 2015. (E-book)

Utkal Dipika. Cuttack, 11 August 1866.

Utkal Dipika. Cuttack, 25 October 1919.

Utkal Dipika. Cuttack, 2 January 1932.

odiabibhaba.in (web)

Error! Hyperlink reference not valid. (web)

www.nuaodisha.com/eminent-personalities/ Gopabandhu-Das.aspx (web)

https://www.collinsdictionary.com (web)

https://en.oxforddictionaries.com (web)

https://travelthemes.in/post-independence-of-orissa/ (web)

https://www.iep.utm.edu/republic/ (web)

https://www.collinsdictionary.com/dictionary/ english/public-intellectual (web)

SOURCES

https://en.oxforddictionaries.com/definition/public-intellectual (web)

...................END..................